MOFFAT
Dumfriesshire

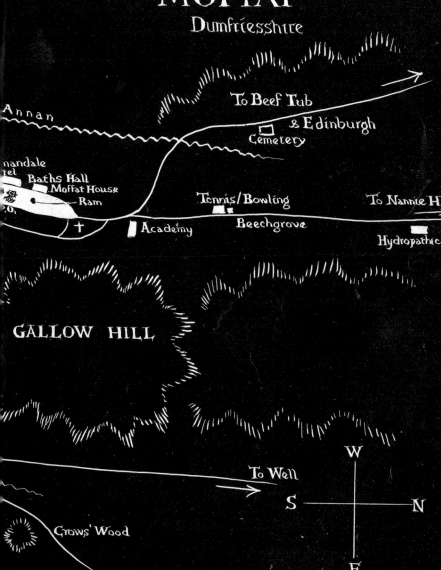

NANNIE

NANNIE
A Lifetime of Devotion

Mora Dickson

LOCHAR PUBLISHING   **MOFFAT · SCOTLAND**

©Mora Dickson, 1988
Published by Lochar Publishing Ltd
Bankhead
Annan Water
MOFFAT
DG10 9LS
Tel: 0683-20916

British Library Cataloguing in Publication Data
Dickson, Mora
    Nannie: a lifetime of devotion
    1. Scotland. Social life, 1910–1936–
    Biographies
    I. Title
    941.1083'0924

ISBN 0-948403-06-3

The publisher acknowledges subsidy from the Scottish Arts Council
towards the publication of this volume

Designed by Paul Minns
Illustrations by Mora Dickson

Photoset in 10½ on 12pt Bembo by Hewer Text, Edinburgh and
printed by Biddles Ltd, Guildford.

Contents

In memory of Nannie
– whose one regret, I believe, was
that she did not live to see this book.

. . . and that things are not so ill with you and me
as they might have been, is half owing to the number
who lived faithfully a hidden life. . . .

George Eliot: *Middlemarch*

SPRING

Joanna Marshall, who was to become my Nannie, rang the doorbell of the Glasgow house ten days after I was born in April 1918. She wore a new grey uniform; beside her on the step was her neatly packed trunk. For five months my mother had searched for a responsible thirty-year old woman to preside over the Hope Robertson nursery which already contained my brother, Robert. Joanna Marshall was only twenty-two and had never had sole charge of a baby before; but she was confident and determined, with a good training behind her, both at home and as an undernurse.

My mother, who had been in bed with influenza at the time of the first interview, recognised in her a young woman to whom she could entrust the care of much – loved babies with the assurance that her confidence would not be abused. It was important that this should be so. My father had had a bad breakdown and was still in precarious health, demanding much of his wife's attention. The family was about to move into the country away from the fogs and stresses of the city. There would be a new home to set up, as well as a new baby to cope with – and a different way of life with which to come to terms. My mother's concern was that everything should run peacefully and smoothly. She told the young woman in front of her that she would be expected to carry full responsibility for the welfare of the children. Joanna Marshall, strong willed and ambitious to achieve the full status of 'Nannie', accepted the challenge. She looked forward to being entitled to change her name to that of 'her' family, as other girls looked forward to changing theirs at matrimony. She was to get a grey uniform, £34 a year and her meals carried upstairs by the maids. When the Glasgow door opened that April day Joanna Marshall became Nannie Hope Robertson – more familiarly to friends and fellow practitioners – Nannie HR.

Born on 11 January 1896 at Stenhousemuir, Joanna was the fourth of nine children – eight of them girls. Her father George Marshall was a foreman grinder at the Carron Iron Works near Falkirk in Stirlingshire. He was a hard-working, much respected member of his community, looked up to by his workmates, loved and admired by his children. A scrupulously fair man in all his dealings, George Marshall was determined that each child would have the same chance to find a place in the world. To this end he set aside, in exact equal parts, the amount of financial assistance he could afford to give them. His wages amounted to £2 a week.

Margaret Marshall was a Ure, a family which had produced distinguished men including a Lord Advocate for Scotland, the first Lord Strathclyde. She worked for a tailoring business in Stenhousemuir. Her craft was to make whaleboned evening dresses and she was a meticulous and beautiful seamstress. Money was never plentiful in the Marshall household, but skill and patience and creative ability abounded: as did pride in standards maintained and time well used. Joanna inherited many of her mother's gifts, and the determined spirit that ensured good use of them. As each of the girls left school at fourteen they spent some time at home, receiving a thorough training in the domestic arts and in the care of smaller sisters before they moved out into a wider sphere.

Joanna herself had had very little formal education. About the time when she was ready to accompany her brother and sisters to High School, George Marshall acquired a house in Larbert overlooking the railway. This became their permanent home. But in her first year at school Joanna contracted a rare fever which resulted in long months of illness and the loss of her greatest physical asset, her beautiful brown hair. Fortunately the hair grew in again, but its owner had no more schooling until she was eleven and a village school was built in Larbert – perhaps because the mile walk with her siblings to the High School was considered too much for her. Maybe this extra time at home contributed to the exceptional development of her household talents. However, at fourteen when her compulsory education was over, her father insisted on her going for a while to night school, where she won first prize for sewing against stiff adult competition.

When she was eighteen Joanna Marshall got the chance of an excellent opening in England. If it had not been so promising George Marshall might have been reluctant to let her go. But she was a sensible, capable girl and as a start in life, though distant, it could hardly have been better.

The Marshalls' next door neighbours had a cousin, who was Nanny to an eminent family in the south, who sometimes came up to Scotland for her holiday. In 1913 she happened to mention that she was in need of an undernurse and, in no time at all, Joanna was engaged at £12 a year, plus uniform. It must have been a daunting, as well as an exciting moment when she stepped out of her home and the small community in which she had always lived, to set off with her father to catch the train to London.

Her situation was to be that of third nurse in an establishment of twenty-two staff. The job might have come to her through known neighbours, but the London Nanny had so little knowledge of her new underling that Joanna had to wear a cerise feather in her hat to ensure recognition at the station. The colour of the feather offended her taste and made her feel disagreeably conspicuous. Her father gave a florin, two shillings – a considerable proportion of his week's wages – to the guard, so that he would keep a watch on the girl during the long railway journey.

The London family was affluent; the nursery large and well run. Nanny was strict but humane, and she took the training of her undernurses seriously. There was a cheerful camaraderie among the young staff and enjoyable nursery outings. One of the five family cars, driven by the third butler, was always at Nanny's disposal for the nursery party. When war broke out in August 1914 they all went down to the country estate in Buckinghamshire, where fruiting trees in the cherry orchard were hung with alarm clocks to frighten off the birds. Joanna enjoyed herself, and learned the elements of what was to become her vocation. She would gladly have stayed had it not been that George Marshall, disturbed by the outbreak of hostilities, wanted his daughter back nearer home.

She found a position, still as undernurse, with a family in Glasgow. Once again it was a happy experience. But she was conscious now of her own abilities and ambitions. At twenty-one she decided to look for a situation where she would be 'Nannie', in full charge. The Glasgow family were sorry to see her go, but they understood her motives – and were to remain lifelong friends.

The step into independence was not, at first, a success. It was true that she had now moved up to £24 a year and had the full responsibility for a small girl of eighteen months. But outside the nursery things were not so satisfactory. The child's father had a roving eye and Joanna soon found herself uneasily aware that she was not exempt from his attentions. Part of the Nannie's code was an unwritten rule that parents did not come into the nurseries after 10.00pm. When Joanna discovered that the key of the night nursery door had been quietly extracted, she recognised that her authority was being tampered with – and suspected that her person too might be in some danger. Though innocent, she was not entirely ignorant. She told her mistress that the key must be returned; then found it in a jar outside the nursery premises. It was reinstated, but very soon went missing again and this time the keyhole was blocked up.

Joanna wrote home to her mother; it was one thing to suspect what might be going to happen, but quite another to be able to put the vital message into plain words. Her mother replied that George Marshall said his daughter was to stick to her post. He felt certain that she was just lonely, missing the company of the large nurseries that she had become used to. Joanna recognised that the failure was hers. She knew quite well what her father's response would have been if he had really understood the reasons behind her uneasiness.

So, on her own initiative, she handed in her notice. It was not accepted. 'Just take a holiday', her mistress said, 'You'll be all right'; though she must have known very well the difficulty with which her young Nannie contended. Or perhaps she hoped that her husband's roving eye would soon be engaged elsewhere.

So Joanna took her holiday, and face to face with her mother was able to put the sorry tale sufficiently clearly. Her mother told George Marshall, who instantly exclaimed, 'But you should have brought your bags with you!' Courageously, she went back and collected her luggage.

Her next place, in charge of two small girls, was no more successful. It lasted six months, during which time she discovered that her new mistress suffered from mental aberrations which presently took her into a nursing home where she died.

Joanna, temporarily as undernurse, returned to the Glasgow family from whose nursery she had first stepped out to plough an independent furrow. They were delighted to have her, but she must herself have been conscious of failure. So when news of my mother's advertisement reached her, and discreet enquiries seemed to show that this was likely to be a place in which she would be treated with decency and respect, it was a matter of great importance to her that the first interview with this new employer should go well. When it became clear that the responsibilities to be undertaken could be more onerous than was usual, for my mother said frankly that there might be times when she would have to devote herself entirely to my father, Joanna's spirit might well have quailed. There was to be no nursery maid, and in the families in which she had first learned her craft nursery maids were an essential fact of life. Sole charge of a small boy of two and a half and a new baby was no light undertaking in the most favourable circumstances; to start work in a nursery already poised for removal, with future accommodation unseen, added to the uncertainties of the situation. But Joanna had not yet made the successful transition from junior to senior status. She saw this as her opportunity and was glad to grasp it.

When, in the May sunshine, Joanna Marshall first carried me out for an airing in the Botanic Gardens – the pram having already gone to the country – she had no qualms about being conspicuous, and hoped indeed that all eyes were upon her. She wore the new grey costume; my mother had cut up her own wedding dress to make me a long satin coat – for both of us it was the start of a long association. For Nannie HR it was a moment of supreme pride.

★   ★   ★

My mother was also one of a large family. Of thirteen brothers and sisters she was the eighth and she had often wished that she had been born a boy. Proud of the physical achievements of the two brothers next in age, she longed to emulate them; and indeed in the sports to which clinging skirts allowed her access, golf, skating and cycling, she did. She was strong willed, energetic and possessive; because of her temperament and the presence in her own family of three older sisters, she had gone into marriage almost totally ignorant of the mechanics of running a household. But she knew very well what she wanted. She had a decorative flair, an instinct for the dramatic and the talent to create a happy home. She had also, as had my father, an active social conscience. He was a man whom everybody loved; generous, open to all appeals, with a heart on which the cares and sorrows of other human beings weighed heavily. He was also tremendous fun. But the armour, which we all of us grow to turn aside the arrows of life, was, in his case, singularly thin, and many who knew him felt an instinct to protect him – not least my mother and, in time, Nannie HR.

In the summer of 1918 the family left Glasgow and moved sixty miles south to Moffat, which was to be our home for the next thirty-two years. It was a small country town lying in the hollow of rolling hills, twenty-one miles north of Dumfries from which the county took its name. Looking down from the lip of the Devil's Beef Tub, where the road from Edinburgh left the bleak uplands and began to descend into Annandale, the town appeared compact and cosy under the wooded slopes of Gallow Hill. The square steeple of the Parish Church focused its aspirations skywards. Trains, emerging from the river valley two miles to the west, whistled as they roared past Beattock Station towards England. From the green heights on a summer day Moffat looked a safe, quiet place, no longer involved in the fears and passions of the past, the torments and struggles that had named some of the features of the land and built the stone watch tower that guarded the Beattock road. It was a well set up, respectable place drowsing in the evening sunshine after a good day's work; though just as often it lay almost hidden from the home-comer by a soft smirr of unremitting rain.

Nannie

Moffat from the south

Moffat was genteel; in a mild way it functioned as a spa, having a Baths Hall where the sulphurous water from a hill spring could be drunk – if those who sought its curative assistance did not feel able to walk the two or three miles to the source. Once there had been a time when coaches brought seekers after health especially to Moffat to benefit from this well water. The town was the centre of a farming community, a thriving nucleus of small tradespeople and shopkeepers, with a Hydropathic, two reputable boys' preparatory schools and a variety of churches. It was a country very different from the central industrial belt of Scotland, with its coal mines and flaring iron furnaces, that had lain in the background of Nannie's youth; and from the busy foggy city which had, up till now, been home for my mother and father.

There were no more reivers driving stolen cattle up from the south into the shelter of the great bowl of the Beef Tub, or hunted Covenanters skulking in the wide open spaces of the moorlands beyond; even the broad High Street, headed by the handsome statue of a Ram, never now saw a sheep market, but human nature being what it is the pains, passions and pleasures of life survived in Moffat all the same.

We moved into a rented house called Ardenholm. It stood outside the town centre, past the school playing fields and over a crossroads, by a group of small houses and a branch post office known as Holmend. A little further on was the

8

cottage hospital, in which my mother was to take a great interest, and Rogermoor Farm which became the focus of many of our nursery expeditions.

But the arrival from Glasgow, which Nannie had looked forward to as the real start of her independent career, was marred by a severe challenge to her skill and devotion. Her baby, myself, whom she had so proudly and publicly displayed, had caught an infection which covered my head with boils and filled the household with anxiety. For four months, day and night, Nannie fought to give aid and comfort to a fragile bundle with its skull, under a tiny bonnet, covered in cotton wool. At night she tied a pillow to her arm and sat in a chair in the day nursery with the baby on her lap, to allow my three-year old brother to sleep undisturbed. At last, obeying the natural law that so often reserves those moments just before the tide turns for the blackest and most dangerous assaults of the storm, there came a particularly bad night. In the morning my mother and Nannie, who had sat up together through the hours of darkness, put the baby in her pram and wheeled her down to the doctor. He lanced a swollen gland and I began to recover. Before this moment, however, the crisis had provided Nannie with her first nursery maid.

There were to be many difficult times between Nannie and my mother in their life together, but devotion to their babies – and to my father – united them. This emergency, at such an early stage in their relationship, cemented a partnership that with calmer times might have shown greater signs of strain. There was too an element of necessity on either side. It was important for Nannie that the third attempt at independence be successful; and my mother, whose first priority was to make for my father the kind of home that would protect and support his uncertain health, needed someone absolutely trustworthy in her nursery.

Both Nannie and my mother were women of strong mind. Each knew her place and guarded its limits jealously. When there were differences of opinion, each tended to think that she alone was right. My mother would state her view firmly; Nannie merely became mutely active. Power was on my mother's side; but Nannie could be stubborn and ultimately indispensable. She was a highly skilled practical perfectionist.

Nursery routine at Ardenholm soon became established. Nannie knew how she wished to organise her domain, and for the most part my mother willingly agreed to any practical requests she put forward. Once fixed the daily programme settled into placid conformity. The lines of demarcation between kitchen, tablemaid's pantry, nursery and drawing room were clearly drawn. So too were those between Nannie and the nursery maid. Until I was one year old Nannie prepared my baby food over a gas ring in the nursery, while the nursery maid carried up the rest of the meals from the kitchen. After breakfast my brother went down to the parlour for household prayers with our parents and the maids, while Nannie bathed and dressed me. Perhaps the constant presence of nursery chores explained why Nannie's spiritual welfare seemed somehow, both then and later, to separate itself from the rest of the family.

Once the nurseries – always tailor-made and in the plural – had been cleaned and the nursery jobs meticulously accomplished, with Nannie keeping a sharp eye on the way those subordinate to her did their work, we were taken out for a walk. Nannie was very small, with rather protuberant brown eyes in a full round face. Her one physical vanity was her mass of beautiful brown hair. She had another, more subtle, conceit centred in her pride in the well-being and appearance of the children under her care. When we went out with her both she and we, and no doubt the nursery maid too, were as immaculately turned out as it was possible to be. But Nannie was young and in love with her job and the countryside in which she found herself, and she enjoyed those walks up to the farm to see the lambs and chickens, or down to the town, as much as we must have done.

In the afternoons, after lunch and a rest, she took us out

again – perhaps on a more adventurous outing such as a joy ride to the Well in a pony cart. Then we came home to tea and were once more washed, dressed and inspected before the highlight of the day, the hour from five to six downstairs in the drawing room with our parents, from which Nannie sometimes received us back with clucks of disapproval at the state into which we had been allowed to get.

This regular routine was punctuated by parental visits to the nursery, where Nannie made plain what was to be permitted, as opposed to the time downstairs over which she had no jurisdiction. Often it was my father who came, full of games and jokes, enjoying the peaceful nursery atmosphere which made no demands on him. He could always find a way round Nannie's strong sense of what was fitting, and when he particularily wished to cozen her he used to call her 'Nurse', which though a less prestigious title than 'Nannie' in her eyes nevertheless carried overtones of flattering superiority. Nannie treated my father's visits to the nursery as she would have those of another child: when my mother came it was a meeting of equals, warily watching each other for any infringement of the unwritten rules that governed their relationship.

Nannie had no great opinion of my mother's domestic talents, but in one area there was a degree of mutual respect. My mother could embroider and Nannie made no claims for her own skill in this kind of work: Nannie was a beautiful seamstress with no rival in the family, but she was willing to admit that my mother also sewed well. For my first Christmas present Nannie made for me a complete, feather-stitched, layette for a baby doll. Sixty-three years later, carefully preserved by Nannie herself, it was to be exhibited to an amazed primary school class, whose conception of the clothing worn by tiny infants was bounded by jumpsuits and jeans, and who had never heard of barries or binders, or seen long flannelette vests.

This peaceful life was, however, occasionally interrupted by more dramatic incidents. One morning Nannie, brushing my hair, heard loud screams. She thought that something had happened to my brother Robert on his way back from parlour prayers, but when she opened the nursery door all was quiet. No sooner had she shut it again than the screams erupted louder than before. They came from the bathroom.

Leaving me, Nannie rushed to see what was happening. At the foot of the stairs father and mother also started to the rescue. Seeing a chance for exploration, I toddled through the open nursery door. In the bathroom Robert, who as he passed had seen the maid cleaning the bath and been unable to resist the temptation of creeping up behind her, seizing her legs and tipping her in, was both delighted and alarmed at the results of his enterprise. Nannie, uncertain whether to admonish him or silence the screeching maid, was riveted in her tracks by the sounds of a second screaming. Bouncing fatly like a soft rubber ball I had rolled down the stairs to the intervening landing. Being at that stage of my life well padded I took no harm. Nannie remembered it as a most exciting morning, and no doubt my brother was given temporary cause to regret his actions.

The alarm in the night was more serious. It happened when I was only a few months old. The nurseries were equipped with the latest in floor covering, a warm linoleum made of cork which had to be polished with a mixture of beeswax and turpentine made up in the house by the maids. Beside the grate the night nursery had a gas ring loosely joined on to a rubber pipe.

At 10.00pm Nannie heated my last bottle on the gas ring, fed me and went to bed. She woke at midnight to see, with horror, that the draperies on my cot were ablaze. Without hesitation she snatched me from the circle of fire and flung me on to her own bed. I had not made a sound. In the other bed Robert slept quietly. Seizing something to smother the fire Nannie crushed it out, took me in beside her and again composed herself for sleep.

In the morning the damage was plain. Not only were the draperies destroyed, the paint on the cot had blistered and peeled. At 7.00am Nannie's cup of tea arrived, brought by a maid who goggled and was told sharply that she was to hold her tongue until Nannie herself was able to break the news to my mother.

It was thought that a smouldering thread of unabsorbed polish must have crept across the linoleum from the gas ring until it found the flimsy, floor length muslin around the cot. Nannie herself hardly knew how she had coped, only that the demand upon her had been instant, giving no time for hesitation, presenting an immediate threat to the welfare of her charges. My mother may have had more ambivalent feelings, post-incident horrors combined with a sense that she had been by-passed in a situation which might have ended catastrophically. She had delegated the responsibility that Nannie carried, but the exercise of it was sometimes another matter.

The calm with which Nannie dealt with an emergency which might well have sent more experienced women crying for help filled my father with admiration. 'Wee Nannie', he said, 'who was frightened even for a mouse'. He grossly underestimated her, but at that time he hardly knew her. Mice might have her standing on a chair, but the real trials always found her fully in control. But I grew up with an unnatural terror of fire, which was not assuaged until I discovered late in middle age the trauma that had caused it.

In the cold winter of 1921, in January, my brother Laurence was born and the inmates of Nannie's nursery extended to three. My mother had been uncertain as to whether it might not be better for my father to be absent over the time of the birth, but he was determined to be there. On a bitter night, with snow on the ground, Cook was roused to light the range and put on pails of water to heat. My father took out the car and went for the doctor and the nurse. An excellent maternity nurse had been engaged, but at the last moment she had been unable to come and her substitute was not efficient and nearly had a disastrous effect on the new baby's digestive system. Told to dilute his bottle with barley water, she gave him thick barley soup.

Nannie, inspite of her lack of professional training, must have felt the scornful contempt of the expert practitioner for the bungling amateur. When she was fifteen she had after all been handed her own youngest sister by the midwife, directly after the birth, and been told to look after her.

It was to be a bad year. The baby was sickly and needed constant care. The following winter there was a virulent influenza epidemic. In Glasgow, at the family home for Christmas, my father took it. Then my mother succumbed, to lie very ill in the care of two nurses. Presently they also caught the virus and left. They were replaced, but the 'flu continued to rage through the house, striking down all in its path. Even Nannie developed a mild attack. But through the chaos and confusion of a household in turmoil, of sickrooms to be catered for and children to be isolated from infection, Nannie remained quietly and calmly in control. In this crisis my mother's original assessment of her as a young woman who could shoulder responsibility was triumphantly justified. By the time I became conscious of her presence in my life she was an essential part of the family home and already settled into agelessness. It was never to occur to me that she was fifteen years younger than my mother.

$$\star \qquad \star \qquad \star$$

Alastair, the final addition to Nannie's nursery, arrived in 1923. His coming coincided with my own first childhood memory, as it did with my fifth birthday.

My mother lay in the big fourposter bed with its rose silk curtains. Beside her a small girl, dark hair in long, well-trained ringlets arranged over her shoulders, sat upright on a stool with a tea tray in front of her. I was both overawed and proud. Nannie and my brothers were out visiting. My own birthday was imminent and I had been promised a particularly exciting present.

As to the date of this glimpse of the past, my memory and

Nannie's conflicted. Perhaps she was right. Adult reason says that the tea party could hardly have finished at 5.00pm in a peaceful *tête-à-tête* and the baby arrive at 6.15pm, to be handed over to me next morning gift-wrapped in a white shawl. Nevertheless my recollection connects the two events intimately and closely.

The bedroom in which this scene was set did not lie in Ardenholm. The whole family had wanted another girl, but more room was needed to allow for such a contingency so my father bought 'The Lodge'. It was one of three houses up a lane at the edge of the village. A large garden full of trees and bushes surrounded it. At the foot of the lane, on the other side of the road, was the mill pond. When the mill was working the whine of the great circular saw, as it rasped out the long smooth planks and ate its way through the huge round tree trunks, could be heard in our garden.

Nannie had the best room in the house for her day nursery. Parental friends considered this a mistaken sense of priorities in my mother. It was very big, L-shaped, with bow windows facing both west and south. The latter one (as did our parents' bedroom) looked over the flat roof of the wooden drawing room which a previous owner had added. This happy chance enabled Father Christmas, at the appropriate time in full regalia and accompanied by a sledge, to enter the nursery directly from the chilly darkness of a winter's night. In the grate a bright fire normally blazed. Round it a square guard with a padded top which made a broad seat naturally attracted any who came into the room. On either side of the chimney breast the height of the gas lights had been adjusted, by special request of my father, so that Nannie could easily reach them.

The night nurseries were across the landing. There were two, interconnecting, with a couple of steps between. In the outer one I slept, in the inner Nannie with her current babies. Robert had been promoted to a room of his own. In the mornings I used to watch Nannie speculatively as she passed through in some *déshabillé* on her way to the nursery bathroom. She looked surprisingly different when she was untidy.

The big day nursery was at this time our world. Its great bow window mirrored the seasons. In spring the crows cawed raucously as they fought to construct their untidy nests on the most advantageous branches of the huge beech trees that, as yet, were covered by hardly more than a thin veil of green. As the sun set crimson behind the golf course hill the whole colony would fly up suddenly, black against a paling sky, with a noisy clamour of calls and wings before they circled round and settled back for the night. If one came down the nursery chimney, as sometimes happened, Nannie would tell us that it signalled a birth. I do not remember that we ever kept a check on those predictions and, in any case, there was no immediate time limit indicated and our memories were very short.

The west window overlooked the front of the house. Below was the grass slope covered in daffodils down which we rolled hard-boiled Easter eggs. Beyond lay the dark bank of purple flowering rhododendrons that marked the boundary of our territory. We could keep an eye on those who came up the lane behind it, by motor car or horse-drawn vehicle. Or we could watch cyclists leave their machines at the wee gate and walk up the path past the yellow laburnum tree. Nobody told us then that its pods were poisonous. There was also a back path down to the wee gate, which maids, messenger boys and tinkers used, but not, I think, Nannie. In our nursery eyrie it was visible to us as well, and we looked out especially for Walter Beattie who came two days a week to work in the garden.

Wattie had been badly gassed in the war, making a calm outdoor job important for him. He had a thin haunted face and was a man of few words, who ate the midday sandwiches that he brought in a bandana handkerchief in solitude in the greenhouse among his seedlings. In bad weather he sat there ruminating gently with a pipe in his mouth, racked every now and then by coughing. He was a vegetable man, with little use for the frivolity of flowers, though he did his best to satisfy my mother's desire to decorate her house with them. He called Nannie 'Nurse', and kept himself aloof from the affairs of the household. Whatever winds of dissension swept through those who lived indoors, no one disliked or had words with Wattie. Since he had a son of his own, he had a weakness for small boys and was willing to pass on whatever skills – of fishing or whittling, if not of gardening – he possessed.

In summer Wattie laboriously cut the large expanse of grass below the daffodil bank with a hand mower, stopping every now and then to mop his brow with the bandana. We could smell the heady scent through the open nursery window and hear the sniffles of my brother Robert's hay fever and the whine of the mill saw above the intermittent grinding of the lawnmower and the banging of bluebottles trapped between the doubled glass. Sometimes there were plagues of Daddy-Long-Legs, both terrifying with their spidery softness and fascinating because their legs came off so easily. In the summer twilight bats swooped and flitted through the air. Nannie was afraid of them and told horrific stories of what might happen if they got tangled in our hair. She was known to have spent one night completely wrapped up in her sheets when a bat got into her bedroom; and I, as a grown-up, once slept in the bath leaving my own room to a visiting bat. In both cases, mercifully the intruder found its way out by morning.

In bad weather, or in the autumn, when gales were raging out at sea, the seagulls came screaming up from the Solway Firth, their melancholy cries echoing round our house. We knew that this invasion was a warning of the storms that would follow and so sat on the toy box in the window watching the clouds bank up threateningly over the school playing fields. When thunder storms broke around us they could be terrifying, cracking and growling in the heavens, lighting the church steeple with a ghostly glare, hissing through the beech trees like venomous electric snakes. If we could hear the hoot and rumble of the trains as they passed through Beattock station that indicated rain to come, as did the height at which the swallows flew. Then the nursery window, which in summer had seemed too small to encompass the whole entrancing summons of the outside world, suddenly appeared immense and melancholy with its expanses of unremitting rain.

But there were fine days too in the autumn, when the Virginia creeper on the house front blazed in crimson and maroon, the beech trees turned gold, the smoke of Wattie's bonfire beside the greenhouse rose up blue into the sharp air and the swallows gathered in flocks preparing to fly south.

In winter the nursery ceiling became a startlingly pure reflected white when snow lay on the ground. The church steeple and the town roofs, behind a black frieze of trees, were acutely differentiated from an albino landscape by the dark shapes of snow-free walls and the harsh shadows of overhanging gutters. The breath of the milkman's horse rose in clouds as he breasted the slope of the lane. Then we could spy the postman's footmarks coming up the path and the arrow trail of tiny claw prints where the resident robin had searched about for food. We skittled down the daffodil bank on tea trays and built a snowman that we could see from the nursery window, while Nannie worried about whether we were warm enough.

Inside the nursery itself was cosy, at least in so far as a roaring coal fire could make it. In those early years, before electricity arrived, fires were the only heating and outside the radius of their life-giving incandescence the house was often freezing cold. Indeed I used to think that a line dividing hot from cold could be clearly drawn through the human body; in front a delicious glow infused the flesh, behind the arctic temperature sent shivers down the spine. It was a situation ripe for the incubation of chilblains, and one that never failed to bring out a painful crop on my own fingers and toes.

Going to bed, across an icy landing, was an event to be delayed whenever possible, and then undertaken with as much speed as Nannie would permit in the rush to seek the comfort of a rubber hot water bottle – or even the less sensual warmth of a stone 'pig' in a woollie cover. I had ambivalent feelings about the fire in my room, fed by coal carried upstairs by Wattie to the special bunker in the housemaid's pantry. I was unwilling to sleep until it had sunk to an unmoving glow. The reflected flames dancing on the ceiling, a sight which to everyone else brought comfort and the fascination of watching the rosy shapes form and reform, making pictures which stirred the imagination, filled me with nervous forebodings. One night the Hydropathic was burned down and in the agitation surrounding this tragedy, with my father asking Nannie to make up a bundle of clothes for a small girl my own age who had lost everything, I found a reinforcement for my fears. The spectral wail of the siren which summoned Moffat's volunteer fire brigade to action made my flesh creep. My father also had a deep fear of fires. In my bedroom, curled up beneath the window and attached to a strong ringbolt in the floor, lay a substantial rope down which I would be expected to climb if cut off by flames. I do not remember practising this manoeuvre and I sometimes wondered how Nannie would manage if such an emergency ever arose.

The coldest part of the house for us was the long passage that connected the hall downstairs with the built-on wooden drawing room. Each winter evening, while goosepimples came up on our arms, we negotiated it rather slowly with Nannie or the nursery maid to spend the children's hour with our parents. Coming back we rushed through it by ourselves at breakneck speed – as a rule that is! But, in what was after all a very public life, this dark narrow passage could also be a private place. Once I remember Robert took me awkwardly round the shoulders and kissed me clumsily.

However often we might have seen our parents during the day, this drawing room hour, between five and six, was an institution, part of the ritual implicit in having a Nannie at all. The nursery party came in at 4.00pm from its afternoon airing and then, tea over, we were undressed, washed and decked out in clean clothes to go downstairs. Certainly in my case everything came off, knickers, two petticoats – one of them always viyella – vest, socks, shoes. No doubt the sprucing up of my brothers was equally thorough. A great many of those garments, if not most of them, were made by Nannie herself. In a sense we were her showcase, as indeed we were our mother's. Perhaps this applied especially to the only girl in the family, myself. As my brothers passed out of the baby stage they were expected to be boys, with dirty knees, scuffed shoes and a liking for rough games. My mother, after all, had once longed to enjoy all those things herself. But I was to remain a cherished girl, round whom her devotion and my father's, combined with the talents of Nannie, could weave miracles of dainty femininity. The only trouble was that, though I did not rebel, I was neither physically nor by temperament that kind of girl.

Nannie lovingly tended, until it glowed, my naturally straight hair and brushed it round her finger in long ringlets. These had to be sustained by a night time exercise which came close to a minor torture. For every evening the locks were separated and tightly wound up round rags torn from an old sheet, until the whole of my head was covered with knobbly little bundles of hair each sprouting two white flags, like an unusual and exotic cactus plant. Only the fact that I was healthy and tired made sleep at all possible, for to find a clear space on the pillow, and to do so without an excrutiating pull on neighbouring bundles of hair, was often quite beyond my capacities. But I accepted that one must suffer to be a Pears Soap little girl, though I had the most profound reservations as to whether such an end was feasible or to be desired – and in any case we used Wrights Coal Tar Soap in slippery tortoiseshell cakes.

Those bedtime rites started at 6.00pm with Alastair, the youngest, and we followed in due order. The nursery bathroom had a very large bath enclosed in a wooden casing, into which I was often popped with one brother or another.

Nannie, in an enveloping white apron, sat on a stool ready to embrace us in an enormous fluffy towel when she could get us to come out. She washed us with brisk thoroughness, into the ears, behind the ears, between legs and toes, sometimes into the eyes too amid indignant protests from screwed up little faces. Too much nonsense and she pulled up the plug, but she enjoyed my father looking in to joke and play water games and relaxed her vigorous attack on our persons until he had gone. Then muffled in the towel we were rubbed down, if we were constipated laid over her knee and a sliver of soap inserted into our anus – which often seemed to do the trick (more obstinate cases required syrup of figs) and put into our night clothes. After which we knelt down to say our prayers and, clean and peaceful, (except for my rags) were tucked up in bed to await our goodnight kisses.

Just often enough to create an apprehensive watchfulness a huge black beetle fell out of the bathroom towels, or even horror of horrors our discarded vests, knickers or my liberty bodice. They hit the floor with a hard metallic bump, to scuttle away if they were right way up, or if on their backs to lie feebly waving their thin legs in the air. It seemed unfair of them to haunt the bathroom where the small humans they terrorised were usually at a disadvantage when they appeared – being naked; but even if I had my shoes on I never could bear to stamp on the hard-backed glossy creatures. Then they cracked in a sickening way that made their dead carcases almost as revolting as enduring them alive.

After his bath, milk and biscuit, Alastair liked to sit ensconced in a big chair and ask Nannie for a bedtime story. It was always the same one, what had his brothers been doing in the years before he was born. He seemed to feel that he had time to make up; that somehow they had gained an unfair advantage on him. Then, when we were all safely in bed, Nannie and the nursery maid sat down in peace to the best meal of the day.

When it was over, if my parents were having a dinner

party, Nannie, who had an ear for music, used to sit on the stairs and listen to the singing in the drawing room. My father had a good voice and guests, if they had any talent, brought their music. We knew that one, the bank manager's very large wife, caused my father considerable anguish. She had little musical feeling, but on each occasion he was too kind hearted to let her leave the piano without a fulsome compliment. My mother scorned his softness; and the next time an invitation was issued he waited with nervous apprehension to see whether Mrs K arrived carrying the rolled up score of her operatic offering. She always did.

*   *   *

Perhaps unfortunately for him Alastair was endowed with angelic infant looks, which somehow gave substance to the wish we had all shared before his birth that he should be a girl. In fact he was a robust and often naughty little boy. But to match the gold curls that rioted over his head my mother and Nannie designed and made little suits in the same material as my frocks, and dressed him in the ways that would most enhance his appearance. He was a cheerful, good tempered child, but by two and a half he was tired of the exclamations of astonishment that greeted his arrival among visitors and the doubts so often cast upon his masculinity. For him the bald head of one of our uncles represented the acme of male beauty. His desire to emulate this paragon very nearly had a disastrous effect on Nannie's heart.

In the afternoon we had to rest for an hour, or sit quietly and read, as much to give the adults around us some respite as to recuperate our own energies. Alastair did not greatly care for this enforced stillness and usually broke it in cunning ways, devised to be perfectly legitimate. One afternoon all was unnaturally still in the night nursery. Indeed long after the rest was officially finished nothing stirred there. At last Nannie decided to see whether he was still asleep. She opened the door and nearly fell down the two steps within it at the sight which met her eyes. Sitting on the bed, a triumphant smile on his face, holding a pair of scissors and surrounded by a drift of spun-gold locks, a little monster like a plucked chicken grinned up at her and announced, 'I'm Uncle Archie'.

The shock was devastating. Without warning she had lost her beautiful baby with its crowning glory and gained a rascal who had somehow acquired a pair of scissors to which he should never have had access. How could she break it to my mother; what would her reaction be? In this case Nannie herself might well be blamed. It was the end of an era, and for a moment her heart literally misgave her.

My mother was equally shaken. What made it worse was that this act of human vandalism took place very close to an aunt's wedding in which Laurence and I were to have starring roles – I as a bridesmaid, he as a page. Alastair was to appear in one of Nannie's masterpieces, a suit of sky blue silk, his aureole of curls burnished until it shone. It was no doubt the dress rehearsals for this event that had finally convinced him of the need for action.

He was despatched, in Nannie's care because my mother found it too painful and perhaps also as her punishment, to the hairdresser in Dumfries. That he was sent out of Moffat was a sign of the seriousness of the situation. Everything possible must be done to ensure respectability for the big day, even if all semblance of ordinary childish humanity was lost. The sky-blue suit was laid aside for ever in tissue paper, and Nannie now took time off from rolling my hair in rags to rub vaseline into Alastair's bald poll. Engaged in these activities she was not tender. She brushed and brushed the poor wispy remnants that protruded from it until he must have wished that he had left well alone. When she was not doing that she made him another suit, his first real boy's suit, and a small close cap.

He was not displeased with himself, and he had a lively sense of his own importance. He had not wanted to attend the wedding in the guise of a girl, but he did not see why he should not have as well defined a position on such an occasion as we did. Perhaps he particularly resented that Laurence, his companion in mischief, his fellow conspirator in so many ploys both good and bad, should have been picked out to be a page.

'But what am *I* to be?' he asked Nannie, not having found a satisfactory answer anywhere else.

Neatly, giving the word due emphasis, she replied, 'You are most important. You are a *guest*'.

★   ★   ★

About this time, or a little earlier, I went away from home on my own for the first time, to stay the weekend with one of my mother's cousins who had an only child, a little girl. We were the same age and, although I hardly knew her, it was taken for granted that in itself this fact would ensure a successful visit.

It did not. From the moment my parents left me at the door until I returned to the familiar warmth of my own nest, I was miserably, tearfully, constantly homesick. Any idea that I might enjoy the company of another girl never entered my mind. I wanted only my brothers. What my small hostess must have thought of this sniffling, uncommunicative visitor, whom no doubt she had been told to welcome with open arms, I never knew. No return visit was ever suggested and even in later life the remembered horror of that weekend inhibited me from making any overtures of friendship.

Nannie came with me. But somehow, displaced from her own kingdom and as unhappy as I was, she was unable to buoy me up. In fact I had no later recollection of her ever being there. The nursery in which she found herself had alien ways, and with the Nanny who presided over it there was no instant empathy – any more than there was between me and my first cousin once removed. In the evenings, when at least sleep brought consolation for my misery, Nannie sat alone in a strange house – for her counterpart was accustomed to going out when her charge was in bed and had no thought of taking her unwanted visitor with her.

So there we were, each in her own way crying for home, the one openly, the other behind a stiffened upper lip; and the desolation in both our hearts prevented us giving any comfort to each other.

For me the way of life that Nannie had come from to be with us, and sometimes went back to, was of the imagination only. I never remember meeting any of her relatives. I knew that she had sisters, some of whom were married. One had gone to Canada with her husband. There were occasional faint echoes of quarrels with another and once I heard my mother say that she was not surprised, Nannie was a very difficult woman. It must have been a moment when there were differences of opinion in the nursery.

Sometimes Nannie told us of incidents in her own early life; how her father rose at 3.00am to feed some horses on his way to work – whose horses or why we never knew, but it must have brought in a little extra money. Nannie spoke with admiration of her father as she told us how he was respected at Carron, where he was foreman, and of the frequent knocks on the door of the Marshall house which often turned out to be a wife pleading for the reinstatement of a man who had suffered the penalty of being drunk on a machine – instant dismissal. Nannie admired her mother too and, looking round her own spruce nursery with maids and nursery maid to do the rough work, she wondered how Margaret Marshall had managed to cope with her job and her growing family in conditions so much less cushioned. 'I don't know how she did it', Nannie would say. 'On washing day we had a woman, Mrs Finlayson, and then whoever was in the house had to help. There was such a carry-on – all the whites to be boiled and rinsed and all the rest of it.' And of course it was not only the washing, there was ironing, cooking and scrubbing, high standards of cleanliness to be maintained and a constant succession of babies to be looked after. It all seemed a long way from my own protected world, though at the same time, as I could not imagine Nannie young, I took it for granted that she would have performed all those many chores with her usual calmness and efficiency.

Then there were Nannie's nephews and her niece. Once, when I was not there, a small nephew came to stay. On one of her visits to his family he had said to Nannie, 'You never ask me to your house', to which she had replied, 'But I haven't got a house – I stay with a lady. When you're a big boy and can come with Mummy and Daddy you can visit me'.

She intended to put him off, but the next time she went back she was met by her brother-in-law who said, 'You're in for it. He's got his wee case packed.' So he came, and saw where his aunt lived.

Alastair made a reciprocal visit to Nannie's home which he greatly enjoyed. The first morning, remembering how the housemaid took up hot water to our visitors, he enquired when the maid was coming with the brass can and was no doubt delighted when he found that there was no need to wait for any such formal awakening. George Marshall, who used to tease Nannie about her 'birds', because my two other brothers were known at home as Robin and Larks, enjoyed having this third fledgling helping him with odd jobs about the house and garden. Well trained by my father in handling tools, Alastair was deadly insulted when Nannie's sister, on his asking for a hammer, presented him with the little one she used to break toffee. He was a very small boy, but Nannie herself would never have made the mistake of offending him in this way.

Nannie had another nephew who was very clever and always did well at school. He was good at things that were mysteries to me, maths, science and chemistry, and Nannie was very proud of his results. He sounded, and indeed was to prove to be, much cleverer than we were, a fact that used sometimes to puzzle me. As I grew up Nannie's own many talents weighed very little with me in the balance with her lack of formal education. She did supremely well the things I expected Nannies to do well. Though she read Ruby M Ayres, Annie S Swan and *The People's Friend*, I read more widely and voraciously than she did. Curled up in the wing chair, over the high back of which Laurence sometimes preached impassioned sermons to any congregation that he could assemble, I devoured Baroness Orczy, the William books, *Froggie's Little Brother* and anything else I could get my hands on. I thought this an infinitely more worthwhile activity than being able to knit or sew or cook. I considered myself a dunce, but nevertheless more knowledgeable than Nannie – which seemed to me to be in the natural order of things. I thought my brothers supermen with great futures before them and it disconcerted me that Nannie had a nephew who seemed already to have dazzling prospects before they had even started. As a scientist, he was indeed to prove much cleverer than we were. Later, when I arrived at Art College, some of the same confused feelings of my early youth surfaced again when the best student of my year turned out to be a relation of Nannie's, though I had learned by then that talent was no respecter of persons or of backgrounds, and that skilled hands were as valuable as learned heads.

★   ★   ★

Though there were times when Nannie and my mother each suspected themselves betrayed, traduced perhaps, super-seded even, by the other, we children knew very well where the boundaries lay. We respected, though unconsciously, the efforts each made to be fair to the other – especially in times of stress. That there could be any emotional confusion in our reactions to mother and nurse never seemed possible. The intensity of the link between myself and my mother told me that I loved her – and sometimes feared her. I knew the final decisions to be hers. The gentler affection that tied me to

Nannie was often to my shame recognised as discardable; within its orchestration there was nothing of the tuned heart strings on which my mother played. We were well aware too, though we would never have told them so, of their protective roles towards my father.

Once, when my mother was very ill, we discussed our family future if she should die and decided that Nannie would adequately fill the essential function of stepmother. Had either of the two protagonists in this projected scenario become aware of our conversation they would have been horrified – as much at our ability to take stock so calmly in such a potentially fraught situation, as at the sensible solution, which seemed so obvious, from where we stood.

Our own illnesses and ailments were treated at home, if they were minor, by Nannie; if more serious, by Nannie under the direction of our family doctor. The cottage hospital was for altogether more alarming complaints. Large, jovial, with pure white hair over a sallow face – somewhere there was a West Indian connection – the doctor had known us since infancy, indeed he had brought my two younger brothers into the world. He was a man of immense kindness, larded with jokes that we did not always appreciate. His talent for the work of healing was recognised outside the Moffat community. My mother trusted him absolutely, and was indeed to owe her life to him. In the long years that followed his death she was never able to replace him.

A linseed meal poultice was a favourite remedy with both Nannie and my mother; the latter suffered from a chronic bronchial cough and was always afraid that her children might follow in her footsteps. With a deadly hatred I loathed poultices and made heroic efforts to stifle any sign that a winter cold might bring with it a chesty cough. Scarlet in the face, choked with the forced constriction of my epiglottis, I attempted a nonchalant indication that there was nothing the matter; better still, at the first sign of rising phlegm I rushed from the room to hide somewhere soundproof while I hawked and spluttered, returning a few moments later self-consciously composed. It was no use. Nannie was never deceived.

Half an hour after I had gone to bed the door would open. Standing on the threshold, the landing light outlining her hair, was Nannie, in her hands a steaming bowl covered with flannel cloths. My chest was exposed and, high up under my chin, one of the flannels was laid while on top of it a revolting, hot, fluid package, wrapped up in the second flannel, was positioned and tied around to keep it in place. The warmth may have been comforting, but there was something so tactually disgusting about the viscid pulpy mass to which I was unwillingly attached, that my stomach turned. It made no difference. Poultices were popular for many things, upset stomachs, bad backs, incipient aches and pains; sometimes for my mother they were mustard, for us always linseed meal. To the end of their lives Nannie and my mother swore by them; for me getting rid of them was one of the pleasures of growing up.

If it was not a poultice that came round the bedroom door with Nannie it might be a drop of ipecacuanha on a sugar lump to relieve a tickle in the throat. Though sharply unpleasant, this remedy was quickly disposed of – and welcome because it always seemed to work. The most agreeable nostrum was Ponds Extract applied externally to bumps and bruises. It was clear and cold, with a witch-hazelly smell that promised instant restoration. The most chancy and mysterious cures were those applied to warts. From silver nitrate to muttered spells nothing seemed to work, until one day, without any gradual decline, they suddenly disappeared.

For some years, because my father became convinced of the wonderful properties of a cod liver oil cream made in Elgin, we were all subjected to a tablespoonful of the hateful stuff after our midday meal. It looked like mayonnaise and slid down the gullet without difficulty, but the fishy aftertaste made the gorge rise. There was, however, no way of deciding whether the results balanced out the detestation –

and so there were no grounds for appeal. Nannie was implacable, and not averse to pouring it down us if we lacked the courage to be our own executioners. It arrived every month, fresh from the shores of the Moray Firth, and I even suffered the humiliation of being made to take a bottle to school with me.

Measles was our most serious illness. It went through us all. It could be a dangerous disease and we were kept in a darkened room for fear of damage to our eyesight.

But the sequel was enjoyable, though fraught with some possessive qualms. For everything that had come into contact with us had to be fumigated or destroyed. Toys and books that we had played with were burned, sheets, blankets, pillows, curtains, carpets disinfected; floors scrubbed. Then the rooms to which we had been confined were sealed round window and door frames, a small fumigating lamp lit in the centre of the floor and the final spaces stuffed up with paper or rags for twelve hours. There was a strange element to this ritual, the dispossession of rooms so familiar to us, the blocking up of every orifice, walling up who knew what devils to be swept clean by the sweetish smell that filtered weakly through the stopped up keyholes. It was impossible to see what was happening. We could only imagine while we lay, purged, in our strange beds that night, what mysterious act of cleansing was going on behind those closed doors.

The other event that required a ritual cleaning afterwards was the visit of the chimney sweep, probably in the Spring to clear away the thick accumulation of winter soot. Sweeps were lucky, Nannie said, especially at a wedding – as hawthorn blossom was unlucky if brought into the house before a certain date, no clouts to be cast before May was out, a dropped spoon meant a visitor and double spoons on a saucer a wedding. If Nannie could not sleep at night there would be news in the morning.

The nursery had to be prepared for the sweep and his assistant. It was not just depopulated but wrapped up in dustsheets, with the grate opening covered to contain the black, soft powdery falls of debris. The sweep had a large circular brush on a slender rod, to which he added extra lengths as he pushed it up or down the chimney stack. It stuck out at the top like some huge dark aerial thistledown improbably come to rest there. He doffed his cap to Nannie and walked delicately like Agag, but it was impossible to contain completely the feathery lightness of the fine flakes of soot, and even where they had been excluded Nannie's eagle eye detected faint black traces.

Such occasions drove her into a frenzy of activity which affected all around her, especially the nursery maid; and the pleasures of watching the sweep at work were diminished for us by sharp injunctions to 'get out from under my feet'. Her colour heightened, her eyes protruded and a furious energy took over her small body. However long the job took, Nannie never relaxed or put her feet up or had a cup of tea while work remained to be done, and she did not see why anyone else should do so either.

Nannie was a martinet, which perhaps accounted for the fact that nursery maids never lasted long enough to make any impression on me. I remember only Alice Crow, large, cheerful, red-faced and black-haired and probably not easily intimidated; though Nannie showed me a photograph of an earlier one who had deserted us for less privileged children in the city. She did not care for looking after clean children and while Nannie admired her dedication she could not agree with its curious direction. Certainly we were not for her.

Nellie, the housmaid, petite and pretty, called us in the morning with a cup of tea for Nannie. When Alastair and I woke early, he in the night nursery beside Nannie, I next door, maddened by the sun creeping round the edges of the blinds we urged on the languid moments by chanting to each other antiphonally 'Nelly ully up'. It annoyed Nannie and made no difference to Nellie's arrival, but as a defiant liturgy it was splendidly cathartic. The tablemaid was Mary. Tall and stately, she was less fun than Nellie, holding herself aloof, in her own way too a perfectionist. In the stone-

31

floored kitchen Jean held sway. Buxom, with light brown hair, she was a marvellous cook, managing the unwieldy range with flues that needed constant cleaning, well aware of our favourite foods and always ready to give us a welcome. We were the ones who crossed the lines of demarcation, hardly knowing that they were there until a tiff blew up, words were half heard, and we recognised that the time had come to say little and make ourselves inconspicuous.

We did not stay inconspicuous for long. This was our world and we knew that it revolved round us.

SUMMER

At the side of The Lodge, in a corner of the flat square of grass where we played rounders or croquet, grandmother's foot-steps or cricket, searched obsessively for four-leaved clovers and made daisy chains, there was a white painted summer house in which Nannie sat on long sunny afternoons. Sometimes we had nursery tea there – everything tasting quite different though all the ingredients remained the same.

Nannie was never idle. My father and mother lazed outside on deck chairs, or joined in our games as arbiters, referees, the 'home' to which we rushed in the frenzy of hide and seek. Inside the little house Nannie cut and sewed and knitted, keeping us tailor-made and trim, setting on our clothes the distinctive stamp that made other mothers with less talented Nannies envy our mother's access to her skills. She watched us smiling, if crisis loomed, knees were scraped, fingers penetrated by thorns, if we felt sick, fell in Wattie's compost heap or off a bicycle, then Nannie emerged to clean, patch up, medicate and generally set us back on our feet again. Otherwise, although she was with us, if our parents were there she made of the summer house an outdoor nursery with the invisible boundaries of possession clearly recognisable.

The garden held other delights besides the summer house and the croquet lawn. Once among the rhododendron bushes close to the lane, in a musty rustling darkness penetrated by the sweet smell of nearby azaleas, it was possible to hide from Nannie. We would watch her crying to us to come in to tea or bed, or to be cleaned up, and take pleasure in her rising annoyance; until the moment that it became plain that a line would soon be crossed which would make our eventual capitulation an unpleasant experience. We had to come out; she never demeaned herself by searching for us.

Within the line of truncated fir trees, which edged the drive from our gate to where it turned on to the gravel sweep outside the front door, it was possible to have a tree house. Inside the outer covering of thick green there was a spaciousness not present under the rhododendrons. Bare branches, easily climbed, ascended in regular rungs up the trunks and a resinous scent was crushed out from the carpet of dried needles. The only trouble was that, once up the tree, it was impossible to see anything and the pleasure of being secluded did not quite outweigh the anguish of not knowing what we might be missing.

At the opposite side of the house from the croquet lawn, on the little back green where the washing flapped and dried, my father, for a time, kept hens. No doubt he thought we would benefit by having our own fresh eggs; though it was easy enough to walk out to Rogermoor and, braving the terrifying, gobbling bubblyjock in the yard, to collect them from the farmer's wife. Our own hens did not prove a successful experiment. My parents had a city background and were not natural animal keepers. Wattie kept himself strictly aloof. Although we became knowledgeable about Rhode Island Reds and Wyandotts, I do not think Nannie cared for the hens. They were messy and quite undisciplined birds and they never flourished. Their wired enclosure quickly lost its initial greenness and became a threadbare, filthy space, scratched over until it offered little of sight or substance to man or bird. It smelled too, and the hens pined and plucked each other bare. But it was enjoyable to go into the henhouse, amid the dust and squawking of disturbed birds, and pick out the warm brown eggs from the straw nests, or to set the china decoy egg under some reluctant layer to trick her into feeling broody. And while they lasted the hens provided the instant supply of raw eggs that the doctor recommended for my mother, and the eggs switched up in milk that Nannie made for my father – both of which remedies we thought disgusting. Before the laying season ended the great preserving pails were taken out and dozens of eggs, mostly after all from Rogermoor Farm, were laid down, circle upon circle, in waterglass to keep us going through the winter.

Behind the hen house, which later became an aviary for my brothers' budgerigars, lay Wattie's vegetable garden, rows of strawberries and raspberries, cabbages, lettuces and sprouts. It was the strawberries that interested us most and when the nets went up to keep the greedy quarrelling birds out, we began to anticipate the days when we would be allowed to go under them. We were good pickers because we were small and near the ground, but better eaters. Wattie was jealous of his fruit and vegetables, and only when our mother was there were we permitted to touch them. Even my mother, in fact, was not always welcome in the vegetable patch.

Across the back of the house a formal flower garden never quite rioted – as I believe we all thought it should – with flowers. Nannie could have made a paradise of it – but neither she nor we had yet discovered her green fingers, and Wattie cultivated plants as a duty and without love. Our own little strips of earth, on the other side of the railings which edged the flower garden, were equally unloved. I never remember the ground there producing anything except the occasional surprised flowering bulb or primrose plant, orphaned in a harsh uncaring world.

Behind the croquet lawn Wattie's greenhouse and the old stables – now the garage – made a huddle of outbuildings in one of which my father had his workshop. He was a good carpenter, determined that his sons should learn early how to handle tools. With their help he made an Indian canoe with painted paddles, stretched canvas on a fine ribbed frame, which was launched one day with appropriate ceremony on the mill pond. Under the huge beech tree beside the workshop Laurence and Alastair made themselves a tented encampment – more gypsy than Indian – in which they attempted to cook appetising messes on a small stick fire. It was the kind of activity watched by my mother and Nannie from different viewpoints. The former enjoyed the unorganised efforts of two little boys pretending that they were living in the wild; the latter thought of all the cleaning up that would eventually fall to her lot and restrained herself, with some difficulty, from interfering.

Within the house Nannie now occupied a position of supreme importance. Maids and nursery maids might come and go, but she was the rock round which the family revolved. If tempers were roused between her and my mother and words exchanged, the thought that she might leave us greatly agitated my father. His was a softer nature than either that of his wife or Nannie, both of whom could assess more accurately the exact degree of tolerance that such differences of opinion allowed. When he made his disturbance plain ranks were once again closed, the lines of interdependence further tightened.

In the village too Nannie had her place, as subtly and as

clearly defined as within the house. When, clean and dressed for show, we walked down the lane with her and turned right towards the town most of its lineaments were as well known to us as the landmarks of our own garden. We knew too of the feuds and which side our mother was on; our father could usually find something to be said for everybody. Moffat might look a homogeneous community but below the surface seethed the communal feelings and failings that any close-knit society is heir to, and there were few who did not find themselves at some time involved in conflict or recrimination, none the less bitter for being conducted behind a facade of courteous self-control. Perhaps Nannie was one of these few not actively engaged. It must have been assumed that, just as she had taken on the family name so she had embraced the family opinions and prejudices.

She never indicated otherwise, though I cannot believe that this was always so. But Nannie was a professional to her finger tips; acutely aware of the things that belonged to her dignity and ours. Her discretion was absolute. She was immensely well informed, but she never gossiped. As representative of the family she knew exactly those to whom she could condescend, those who for our sake were ready to treat her with friendly consideration and, somewhere in the middle, those whom she met on equal ground of friendship or respect.

At the foot of our lane the mill pond was always a source of interest – but not to be explored if we were officially on parade. Once a home-made boat, with brothers in it, sank within a few paddle strokes of the bank, unlike the triumphant launching of the Indian canoe. The humiliation of having to walk home dripping pond weed and mud was greater than the discomfort.

On the other side of the road were the two Floral Cottages, one of which had for a short time housed a missionary aunt and uncle forced to leave India suddenly after communal disturbances. Opposite, Tom Hood, the photographer, had a small makeshift wooden studio on a tiny section of land carved out from the saw mill behind it. He camped out with his wife in what living space remained in the miniature building. Tom wore a beret and rode about on a bicycle, his box-like apparatus balanced behind him. We knew him quite well and it was fun to try to identify the stiff sepia pictures in his window. Once, though the putting of us on public display was not entirely approved of, we appeared there ourselves. Polished up by Nannie, we had sat in front of his tripod camera with the black velvet cover which he draped over his head while he peered at us through the lens. We were encouraged to keep still while one of his hands, broken loose from the enveloping cloth, waved in front of our solemn faces and he implored us to watch the dickie bird. Was there a dickie bird? Memory, often the great betrayer, actually portrays a yellow toy canary somewhere beside Tom Hood's muffled head and clicking fingers.

But it was really the saw mill that fascinated us. It was run by Taylor and Smith, large jovial men who drove a cart behind a huge brown horse with clanking harness and great hairy feet. Used for transporting wood, this waggon also sometimes clattered up our lane with packages from the station. If the mill was operating, the wood smell, the flying sawdust and the concentrated, high-pitched whine of the circular saw all added to the impression of power and drama. In this case it required sharp orders on Nannie's part to move my brothers on.

The smithy lay across the yard behind the *Black Bull*, an Inn since 1568, a public house of ill repute in our twentieth century family. Its claim to fame was that Robbie Burns had scratched a verse on one of its windows with a diamond ring. Of course we never went inside to find out whether or not this was true. At the smithy we could sometimes see the mill horse being shod. Or the much smaller animal that pulled the milk cart and gave a number of boys the illusion that they were imitating Jehu simply by following the stop/start ritual of the milk round which he knew by rote in his horsy heart.

The smithy was dark, with the red glare of the furnace

lighting up the corners when the bellows intensified the incandescence at its glowing core. The horses stamped and snorted. The smith, his leather apron black and shiny with use, manipulated his irons with a craftsman's skill. The red-hot shoe clanged as it hit the anvil, and then slowly faded to pink while the hammer crashed down on it. The smith spoke to the nervy horse with slow reassuring endearments while he caught its great hoof between his knees and clamped the shoe against the horny sole. A hot hissing steam rushed upwards and we shrank back appalled, imagining such an operation on our own tender and tickly feet. But the horse stood stolidly, seeming not to mind, recognising in the smith a creature both knowledgeable and well-intentioned. All this time the smith never looked at us. His craft preoccupied him, and anyway he was accustomed to an audience.

It was down Well Street that most of our shopping was done. Known as Well Road when it passed our lane, the street changed its designation as it neared the town. At the doctor's house on the corner it left the fields behind. After that there were dwellings on both sides, the gates that led up to our church, the tiny hairdresser's shop run by two maiden ladies of uncertain age. At Sinclair's, Well Street began. This large grocer's emporium was presided over by the smooth and obsequious Duncan Mundell. He treated 'Nurse' with deference, finely edged with disdain; her position as representative of a valued customer demanded respect, her personal status he rated well below his own. He was an elder of the Kirk and a noted rumour-monger. But his shop was crowded with all sorts of fascinating goods, including huge bins full of staples, hams and cheeses, budgie food for our birds.

There were two bakers almost opposite one another, Edgar and Hepburn. We patronised them both. The floury new loaves came round from the bakehouse balanced on the Hepburn son's head, on a round flat cloth cushion like one of his own scones. He was a fine upstanding young man, with small roly-poly parents who looked as though they themselves had been fashioned from dough. Mr Edgar, also plump and powdered, carried his own trays of fresh bakings. Sometimes there was a birthday or a wedding cake in his shop window, whose ultimate destination became a matter for speculation – if we did not already know it.

The Provost owned the shoe shop. He was very stately, with a ramrod back and a small grey moustache, a figure more naturally fitted to wear the Council robes than to assist in trying on shoes. His words too were stilted and precise, already honed for the next speech. It did not seem possible to have an ordinary conversation with him. It was a large shop, as befitted a civic dignitary, while on the other side of the road the small general newsagents was the kind of cluttered place in which we could sometimes spend our Saturday penny.

Well Street, being narrow, offered something in the way of a progress, where we could see and be seen. Once in the High Street we were diminished by width and space.

The High Street, which carried the main road from Edinburgh to the south was immensely broad, with two rows of trees in the middle, the red sandstone War Memorial at one end, the grey statue of a Ram on top of the Colvin Fountain at the other. When Moffat had been a spa, and the small ballroom built over the site of the Well echoed to dance music, coaches drew up at the Annandale Hotel to let down their passengers, while at the Balmoral opposite the stage to Edinburgh changed horses before facing the climb up the Beef Tub. Perhaps William Buchanan, who was born in Moffat in 1789, had stepped off just such a coach on his return from the Peninsular Wars having lost a left foot and gained a Chelsea pension.

Once sheep sales had been held in the High Street. The Ram commemorated the wealth on which Moffat had flourished. When we were small there was still an annual fair there – until it was banished to the waste ground behind Andy's garage. Perhaps the Town Council shared Nannie's view that the stalls and hurdy-gurdies brought the gypsies

The
Colvin Fountain,
Moffat

and tinkers who were the bane of her life. They represented a wild, unregulated way of going on – and a dirty one at that – totally at variance with everything she tried to instil into us. If a gypsy came up the front path, boldly selling clothes pegs or white heather, we were hurried out of sight. No one seriously believed that we might be kidnapped, but the myth was strong all the same. The tinkers shambled up the back path to wheedle scraps of food from Jean, leaving cabalistic signs on the gatepost or at the foot of the lane to indicate whether we were a soft touch or not. Once a year a national Motor Rally rushed through Moffat, with a check point in the High Street and the excitement of all night agitation, lights, flares, hurrying bodies and engines revving up. We lived too far away for any of this to impinge on our dreams, but we knew it was there and the tingle of adventure was in the air.

Round the corner of Well Street, where the eighteenth century schoolhouse under its clock tower was now the butcher's shop, we were launched into the open expanses of the High Street. Here our first port of call was likely to be the Toffee Shop, run by the Blacklock family and famous for a particular kind of toffee. The formula remained a close family secret. Twisted strands of glossy chestnut and paler brown toffee were curled into a great round whorl which had to be broken up with a small hammer before it could be eaten. Later, when the tourists began to come, the toffee was made and prepacked in pieces. It never tasted quite the same as when, on the nursery table, we hit the luscious, gleaming coil until it cracked into a hundred fragments and then stuffed the largest one in sight into our open slavering mouths. This sweet had a unique taste and was known far and wide simply as Moffat Toffee. White-haired, black-eyed old Mrs Blacklock would appear from the back of the shop, where the smell of a fresh batch of cooking toffee made the saliva run. She always had some broken bits under her counter to hand out to us, and even Nannie took little persuasion to accept one.

Barr's was a large shop selling china and glass – and also toys. To go in and gaze was exciting enough; if a birthday or Christmas lay just ahead the pleasures of speculation were almost as satisfying as wishes later fulfilled. If we had a little money of our own it was possible to linger over the agonising decisions that had to be made until Nannie got impatient and refused to let us procrastinate any more. It was in Barr's window that I first saw, and lusted over, the Royal Doulton china balloon woman, and for months I never missed an opportunity to stand and gaze longingly at her – until, on one present-giving occasion I found her suddenly in my own possession.

Then we were off up the street to the Post Office, run by Miss Rennie who knew everything about everybody in the town, though it was only rarely – and often accidentally – that she let slip the extent of her knowledge. The Post Office occupied a strategic position on the High Street, opposite the Baths Hall, and though it would have been beneath Miss Rennie's dignity to be seen peering out of its high windows no doubt she satisfied herself occasionally that everything in the village was going as it should. She was hook-nosed with a heavy dark bun, tall and very efficient. Sooner or later the whole town met in her Post Office and exchanged the gossip of the day, with no thought that the postmistress's discreet presence behind the counter was anything more than another manifestation of the official machinery that they had come to use. The Post Office we had in common; other professional or commercial establishments – churches, doctors, banks, grocers, sports clubs – were subject to rivalries and divisions.

The Post Office contained the only public telephone box and it was there, in later years, that my mother first heard that Moffat had become the setting for what was to develop into a notorious murder. A hysterical reporter was shouting down the instrument to his editor that several parcels of human remains wrapped in newspaper had been discovered in a burn up the Beef Tub road by two inoffensive ladies out for a Sunday walk. What incensed my mother in the next months was the knowing look and the comment, 'Ah, the Ruxton murder', whenever she gave her address anywhere out of Moffat.

Down the other end of the High Street, past the Parish Church and the *Black Bull*, the little one or two carriage train that chugged between Moffat and Beattock, two miles away, had its terminus. Taking the short ride was a favourite treat. It had all the feel of a real railway journey, with the engine getting up steam, the whistle blowing, the rhythm of the wheels as they quickened over the sleepers suggesting rhymes to match. The famous advertisement for Ma-za-wa-tee Tea made an admirable chant. While still standing we made faces at the windows to prevent other people getting in to our compartment. Then we opened them and hung out, watching the cows careering away with their tails up, taken by surprise – as they so often were; identifying landmarks as we passed – the Dyke Farm where we skated on the pond, the old Border watch tower and Lochhouse, where my mother used to spend the Easter holidays when she was a child. When we got to Beattock it was fun to wait until a main line train drew in, a larger grander version of our own, and then take on returning passengers for the journey back to Moffat.

Nannie

It was on to this branch line that the Royal Train was shunted to spend the night when the King and Queen were travelling north, a distinction Moffat took personally. Nannie would point out the spot where the old King got out to admire a herd of Belted Galloways, spectacular cows with a broad white swathe round their ample waists cutting through the jet black of their coats. A later Sovereign, less tactfully, was reported to have queried, when told the Provost had called after breakfast to pay his respects, 'Moffat? Where's Moffat?'

Beside the station was the Park, equipped with pavilion, putting green and a pond with boats. It was a trim, well kept park, with ducks and swans nesting on the island in the centre of the lake and plenty of seats for Nannie to sit on while we played around. I think it was probably only with my mother or father that we ever actually went out in a boat. It was not possible to imagine Nannie rowing, and no nursery maid would have been deemed sufficiently responsible to be entrusted with such a task. This, however, did not prevent the water being the centre of attraction and the scene of an occasional accident. We fed the swans with scraps of bread, and fled to the safety of Nannie's skirts when they stretched out their long necks, malevolent black boot-button eyes fixed on us, and attempted to get hold of the crumbs before we had actually let go of them. Or when, in an excess of macho-exhibitionism, two of them reared up on their tails, spread their wings and rushed with a terrifying skittering noise across the surface of the water.

One day Alastair fell in. He was sailing a small wooden boat under a footbridge and, in his anxiety to watch it the whole way through, he stuck his head down almost into the water, overbalanced and fell in. He was fished out, dripping. The rest of us were abandoned to the nursery maid and Nannie, her youngest charge unabashed, but she having sustained something of a shock to her sense of propriety, hurried away up the road and across the High Street towards home and dry clothes.

At the end of Well Street my father passed them in the car and stopped to find out what had happened. Nannie opened the door and prepared to hustle her sopping child inside. My father took one look and refused to have a very wet small son, hung here and there with slimy pondweed, sitting in the motor which was his pride and joy. Both the rejected parties were affronted. Gobbling with indignation, in a manner reminiscent of the bubblyjock at Rogermoor, brown eyes popping, Nannie was forced to complete the journey on foot. In her eyes my father's image took a nasty knock that day, though she tried to justify her failure to twist him round her little finger by declaring that the exercise had been better for my brother.

Each of our walks had its own special features, none of which ever seemed to pall. Though it must often have been wet, windy or dull, in retrospect the weather of our childhood seems more frequently to have been bright with sunshine. I grew up with the knowledge that my body was waterproof, and certainly we all had well used wellington boots, which would seem to indicate – as was indeed the case – that Moffat in its nest of hills had a high rainfall; but of this fact memory has left little trace.

If the small procession, with Nannie in charge, went up the path past our personal gardens and out of our back gate there was a number of options open to it. We could take the long slow climb to the Well where, in a tiny house built over the spring, the sulphur water in a large glass was available for sale. For some time my father, seeking for the physical robustness that evaded him, drank it regularly. To us it tasted like rotten eggs and we could not be persuaded to manage more than a sip. But it was a rare nursery walk that got so far, especially if there was a pram involved. We chanted the rhyme about the road to Babylon, three score miles and ten and winding up hill all the way, searched for flowers in the lush grass verges, said 'boo' from a safe distance to large-eyed cows chewing the cud on the other side of stone walls and turned back to run down the long slope home.

Or we could take the right hand fork before the Well road proper began and stamp over the wooden bridge above a turbulent stream. Then past fields where lambs scampered in Spring and invisible larks sang in the sky to the Crows' Wood. The Crows' Wood was frightening. It was small and circular, its large trees so closely intertwined that once through the gap in the broken-down wall the air was thick with a secret, unfriendly gloom – even in the height of summer. But there was more. The wood had grown up round a mound which covered, so we understood, a Roman fort. Certainly the little hill, with a hollow at its centre, did not look natural – though no archaeologist ever seemed to think it worth investigating – and the wood itself, silent except for the harsh calls of the crows in the tree tops, dank, withdrawn from the living countryside surrounding it, felt haunted.

Nannie remained outside while we went in. But it was an awful place and there was a limit to how much we could stand of the tingling of our nerve ends and the anticipation of some unearthly event.

Less fraught was the walk round the Ballplay, the start of which lay a few hundred yards nearer home across another bridge. The road skirted the tennis courts where my father played and took a wide sweep past the boys' prep school to turn right at the crossroads at Holmend and come back into the village near the police station. We saw the schoolboys, in scarlet jackets, hurrying between buildings, sitting in class-rooms, or playing games in the fields opposite. From the outside they lived a life divorced from the one of which we felt a part. They were a puppet show, put on for our amuse-ment, whose performance closed up during the holidays. Only the headmaster and some of the staff, permanently residing in the town, belonged to the local pantheon that formed the background to our own existence.

At Holmend crossroads we had a choice; to turn left up to the farm at Rogermoor, on the road that led eventually into the hills at the Grey Mare's Tail and over the watershed to St

Mary's Loch, where the statue of James Hogg the Ettrick Shepherd stood gazing out at the dour Border uplands, or we could go straight on to have a look at the duck farm.

If we turned left we passed Wattie's cottage. Sometimes, knocking at the door, we called on Mrs Wattie. Thin and anxious looking, not unlike her husband, she would usher us into her tiny front room, where Wattie might be sitting, silent, fingering his pipe, in much the same way that he sat in our greenhouse. Nannie was given a cup of tea and her children were admired, sometimes recipes or knitting patterns were exchanged, or some sweets, hurriedly acquired from the general shop next door, were handed out to us.

None of us knew what to say and it may be that Wattie's taciturn benevolence, punctuated by coughs, was really the only adequate answer to those unexpected visitations. We knew that he liked us and was prepared to answer any questions that we felt able to formulate. But he did not expect – or offer – light conversation to fill up the gaps. Often it was enough, just to sit on a stool and stare round at the small room, fascinating in its scale so different from our own huge nursery, and at its photographs and ornaments.

Beyond Wattie's house lay Ardenholm, with its tales of the early years when we had lived there before Alastair was born. The sight of it would spark a vein of reminiscence in Nannie and I would try hard to picture myself in those surroundings. But it was always a failure. The little girl, with a pink or white ribbon in her curls, that I saw in my mind was never me but some other well-behaved child out of a story book.

At the end of this road was Rogermoor, where the rooks and seagulls wheeled and squabbled behind the plough or the ripe corn was stooked in sheaves along the fields. Beyond the farm the safe perimeter of Moffat ended and the wilder, less controlled, landscape of the hills began. There was a house called Craigieburn in this outer orbit which was reputed to be haunted. Perfectly ordinary people, like the bank manager, had seen persons in the dress of an older century join an evening party among other Moffat worthies. Set in a hollow surrounded by trees, with the murmur of the Moffat Water running nearby, it was a house made for ghosts. Perhaps the ghosts were made for the house too. There was a widespread belief in Moffat that they existed and going to children's parties in Craigieburn I was always disappointed not to meet them.

Equipped as we were on those nursery walks to be seen and admired, we must sometimes have presented an incongruous sight at Rogermoor Farm with its mucky yard sharp with the smell of manure and the vitality of heavy horses and an imprisoned bellowing bull. In the face of all this rampant life I was often timid, keeping near Nannie's skirts while my brothers, more courageous than me, set out to investigate. But there were hens, of a sufficiently small stature to cause me no uneasiness, scratching and clucking in the midden; and occasionally a scatter of baby chicks doing their best to imitate their Mama and being bawled out by a handsome roistering rooster who had mistaken the time of day. Or even a bottle-fed orphan lamb on a piece of sacking before the kitchen fire, or a couple of unsteady, long legged calves butting with hard little skulls at their mother's stomach. If it was late afternoon we might peer into the byre and watch the milk swish and tinkle into the pail while the dairymaid tugged at their teats and Daisy or Primrose turned a heavy head and gazed placidly at the small human intruders.

The duck farm, which lay at the end of our walk if we went straight on at Holmend crossroads, was owned by Mr Ralston. He loved his ducks, hundreds of white Aylesburys quacking about in pens, paddling in the little burn or sitting placidly on the grass. A rough-haired cheerful man in a polo-neck sweater and long rubber boots with thick knitted stockings folded over the top of them, he would greet us as we passed. Usually he was carrying a pail of food and he smelled of duck and all that went with caring for them. His wife, a pretty frail woman with light hair, beautifully dressed in flowing garments, lived in her immaculate house. There were no children. Each was devoted to the other, but she could not abide the ducks.

Sometimes on this road we met a flock of sheep mee-ing continuously, stirring up dust, their trotters titupping, their harassed white or black faces turning from side to side at the sight of an obstacle to be negotiated or when they sensed the slinking piebald body of the shepherd's dog gently coaxing them on their way. We went every year to the sheepdog trials on the hill behind Beattock station to watch these same nervy animals being cunningly persuaded through gates and round posts by a miraculous communication of cries and whistles between man and dog. The district boasted a famous shepherd of international fame. We all basked in his glory and practised calling 'Come awa tae ma fit' – even though there was no dog to come.

In the autumn there were brambles to be picked, which Nannie made into excellent jelly; at other seasons catkins or pussy willow, harebells, ragged robin or scarlet pimpernel, dog roses, hips and haws, or primroses – the latter to be collected in great drifts and made into bunches to be sold on Primrose Day, which was also Alastair's birthday, 19 April. I made shapeless little floral collections, which died in my hand before I got them home, or we picked buttercups and held them under our chins to see in the reflected yellow sheen which of us liked butter best. I had a passion, which neither Nannie nor my mother shared, for cow parsley, with its delicate lacey flower heads. They thought it a common taste and had no eye for the loveliness of the design.

In the other direction, skirting the northern border of the town and the foot of the Gallow Hill, we took a path through woodland, where red squirrels played in the branches and collected acorns in their miniature hands. This was quite different from the Crows' Wood; here the sun filtered through beech leaves and the undergrowth was light and alive. We looked for bird's nests, parting the branches gently to see if there were any of the eggs which we were taught to admire and conserve. One only could be taken if the nest contained four, and there must be no undue disturbance which might cause the mother to desert her family. The collection was Robert's and we watched in admiration while he made a needle hole in each end of the beautiful fragile shells and blew the contents out on to a saucer.

As it came out of the wood this path meandered between fields, with a view to the south over the town, and glimpses through trees of our own house looking ordinary and unfamiliar when seen from such an angle. Then we climbed a wooden stile into the Crescent, a semi-circle of prosperous stone houses with trim gardens and shining paintwork. The Miss MacClarens, plump, white-haired and kindly, would greet Nannie and ask after our parents. Mrs Goldie-Boag, who tried to disguise what must have been the distorting effects of a stroke under heavy make-up, insisted to our horror on kissing us. She lived alone – with only a goldfish or a budgerigar to talk to, or so we believed – and would have liked to make much of us. With unconscious cruelty we shrank from her and, out of Nannie's hearing, made jokes about her and her name. Then the road ran down a steep hill, past Duncan Mundell's bungalow, where red-haired Mrs Mundell sometimes spoke to us, to join Well Street at the corner opposite her husband's shop.

Or we could go through the town, either by the High Street or the back way past the dentist – whom we did not patronise – and the lanes of little houses to the Wee Free Church which my father, after much heart-searching, had left, and up Beechgrove. Moffat Academy lay on this route and the rival tennis courts. Here too was the bowling green where the Moffat matrons, many of them of tremendous bosom and girth, measured their skills against each other and a number of skinny elderly gentlemen. At the top of this road, before it ran into farmland, the burned-out remains of the Hydropathic still crumbled among its trees.

Once, when I was quite small and Laurence still a baby, the nursery convoy – Nannie, nursery maid, two prams and Robert walking – came on a street organ with a woman turning the handle. Nannie dipped into her purse to find a coin for Robert to give her, so that the monkey would be allowed to perform. The organ grinder, however, refused to take the silver proffered by the small boy and would only accept it from the owner of the purse from which it had been extracted. While the monkey danced to the music, she handed Nannie a fortune printed on a slip of paper. Nannie kept that fortune safely in a drawer until she was well past the age at which it predicted she would die, eighty-three. 'If you want to be really happy you must help others less fortunate than yourself', it said.

★   ★   ★

Although Nannie had friends in the village, we felt her to be entirely and perpetually occupied with our affairs. And perhaps she was. In theory she was entitled to a weekly day off; in practice she rarely took it. All the enjoyment, pleasure and fun of her life was bound up with our family and she was reluctant to leave us even for a day. There may also have been an unacknowledged suspicion in her mind that eight hours' absence might inflict untold damage on the nursery routine if it was left to the tender mercies of the nursery maid; and on our manners and habits if we were abandoned completely to our mother. Sometimes Nannie went down to the Sunday evening service in our church; occasionally she took time off to have a meal with a friend, once or twice she may even have had a friend to tea in the nursery, though this I do not remember. We seem never to have heard young men or followers mentioned. In the years that she had been with us Nannie's work had become her vocation.

There was, however, one group of people with whom Nannie formed lasting relationships. These were other Nannies, professionals like herself, who knew the secrets of the families they served and kept them as she did; with whom she could relax her guard and feel at ease. The Nannie from one of her early positions was already an old friend; in Moffat she found two more.

Nannie

Nannie 'H' and her family lived in a farmhouse right at the end of the Beechgrove road, when it had long ceased to be associated with the town. Outside Beattock, equally far distant, was Nannie 'F's home. Those two families, with one other whose house was beyond Rogermoor, had children of our own ages and were our friends.

It was at the set pieces of our existence that the Nannies met. Three were in the orthodox mould, the fourth, from a family with a vivid energetic Canadian mother, was a very superior Norland Nurse. She wore a formal uniform and worked to rules that the other three considered rigid and almost inhuman. She went by the book, literally, a proceeding that our Nannie thought made few allowances for the variations in nature and temperament between individual children. The fact that she had studied in a College was a matter for disapproval with the other three. The time had not yet come when such an advantage might have resulted in their feeling inferior. Chrissie, the nursery maid in this family, was far more congenial company.

Nannie H, Nannie F and Nannie HR, drawn together by an exclusiveness of caste, a just appreciation of each other's skills, and an ease in each other's company that it was nôt so simple to find elsewhere, grew to be friends. Nannie H was a contemporary of our Nannie, but Nannie F was considerably older. This discrepancy made no difference to their solidarity. The essential agelessness of Nannies, rooted in an inherited craft, transcended barriers. Only Chrissie was allowed to be still young, because she had not yet graduated to the dignity of Nannie status. The Norland Nurse, flaunting her own youth, was altogether a different kettle of fish. The others were already a vanishing breed, though nothing about them indicated that this was so. What rivalries there were, were professional and understood as such. The discretion which was part of their natures, vital to reputation and career, could be circumspectly lowered in the company of those whose discernment of the delicate balance in which they lived their days exactly matched their own. Each spoke of her mistress, I am sure, with the careful judgment of one who knew herself to be the guardian of the family good name – as well as of her own; but at the same time with a wider understanding of the frailties of human nature than those mistresses themselves sometimes demonstrated. It must have been a relief to talk with friends who recognised, and espoused without reservation, the Nannie's point of view.

We all went to dancing classes in the Masonic Hall, quite near to us on the Well Road. It was the Canadian mother, after an attempt at ballet classes had shown up the essentially corporeal nature of the pupils, who persuaded other parents to band together and bring a teacher down from Glasgow to induct us into the mysteries of ballroom dancing. Mothers and Nannies sat round the wall on hard chairs, while the cracked upright piano thumped out two-steps, foxtrots and waltzes and the teacher went 'One-two-three-FAH!' Our Nannie discreetly tapped out the rhythm with her foot. She took trouble with my presentation – hair brushed and ringleted, wrapped in a shawl with my dancing slippers in a shoe bag – no doubt aware that the keen eyes of Nannie F and Nannie H would be upon me, not to speak of the Norland Nurse. Nannie F had only boys under her care, so she was more likely to be nostalgic and admiring than Nannie H, whose one female charge was a wispy little thing. But the Norland Nurse had four girls and, though most of them were tomboys, a critical eye was to be feared.

On me the whole exercise was wasted. I had no musical ear and I loathed the conspicuousness of standing up to dance, convinced that none of the little boys had any reason to want to dance with me. I excepted Robert, who would protect me I knew to the best of his ability, but felt mournfully aware that there were other little girls he might desire to cavort with more; though the truth was that none of the boys showed much interest in dancing at all, until it came to the gallop or the eightsome reel when all the wild instincts of primitive man surfaced in them and they stormed round dragging us with them like captives after a raid. Once I put my foot through the hem of my frock and this seemed to me a disaster of such catastrophic proportions that I had to be led away in floods of tears. It was not that I minded about the dress, but somewhere in my consciousness I had been deeply affected by the loving care lavished upon my clothes by Nannie and my mother and suffered from a depressing sense of my inadequacy as a model for them.

Then there were parties; nursery parties; grander parties organised by our mothers for birthdays, Christmas, Easter, Hallowe'en; grandest of all parties in some of the large country houses of the county. We went to these more often as units in a certain social hierarchy than for friendship's sake, but Nannie greatly enjoyed showing us off in the spacious halls of Auchen Castle, Raehills, Rammerscales and other estates with resounding names. More relaxed were joint picnics or less organised get-togethers in each other's gardens. The latter, and the nursery parties, must have been the easiest for the Nannies. They could compare notes and chat while keeping a perfunctory eye on their charges, or else abdicate altogether for an hour or so in favour of the nursery maid. Even at the larger parties – when mother and Nannie both went with us – Nannie, having seen us safely divested of coats, scarves and shoes, could disappear to the nursery for a quiet domestic cup of tea with her opposite number.

But there was always tension in the air. Would one of us fall into the tub of water when ducking for apples, or eat too much and be sick. And it was known that when in the charge of our mother we were apt to be allowed to get over-excited, requiring a good deal of Nannying before we were returned to our normal state of ordered calm. My mother enjoyed playing games and was herself very good at making them up. Her own parties were splendid ones and she liked to see us throwing ourselves into the enjoyment of other people's. But Nannie never lost sight of possible consequences, and occasionally carried the knowledge that it was she who had to deal with them, too openly upon her face.

★   ★   ★

My father had a series of cars which he enjoyed and eventually, with a good deal of friction, taught my mother to drive. The earliest that I remember was a Minerva, with a brake coming up through the outside footboard on which it was necessary to haul with considerable strength before the desired effect was obtained. Picnics were often whole day outings, from which we came home tired and dirty, replete with sunshine and fresh air – or even shivering and damp – weighed down with treasures, brambles, primroses, stones and shells, great armfuls of bluebells already dying on their thin green and white stalks. It was not always easy to find room in the nursery for these prizes. Back in her own domain Nannie could be impatient of our grubby trophies cluttering up the place.

The Grey Mare's Tail, a tall narrow waterfall whose spume blew out in wispy showers, was a favourite picnic spot. The hill sheep enjoyed our company, coming in single file down the path over the scree to gather round us and accept any spare sandwiches we chose to offer them. They could indeed be uncharacteristically aggressive, stamping on the tin plates and distinctly upsetting Nannie's usually unruffled calm. Lochwood Oaks was another much visited site. There bluebells like torn off bits of Spring sky covered the ground under gnarled trees. Or we went to the Solway coast, where the sea receded beyond the horizon leaving miles of gleaming treacherous sands – and came galloping back again, faster than a man could ride on horseback, to trap the unwary. There were quicksands too, and it was here that witches had once been buried up to the neck to watch their watery death come racing up at them out of the blue.

Nannie was always with us. In the car she sat upright, essentially part of the huggermugger of children, picnic baskets, towels and extra clothes, but at the same time retaining a nursery aura. She wore a hat and looked indulgent, which indeed she was for she loved picnics, but there were limits which neither she nor we crossed. We played car games with our parents. Nannie did not join in.

My younger brothers could tease her, but I do not know that we ever went so far as to perpetrate an April Fool in her vicinity. She always brought her current work with her, never going anywhere without her sewing or knitting, and sat busily occupied, looking sometimes curiously out of place. In itself the occupation domesticated her, under the oak trees, beside the burn, on the sea shore or at the foot of the Grey Mare's Tail. Such a translation of nursery chores made it possible to leave her tending the picnic site, alert for the moment when a splash or a cry might call for her skills as mender, drier, comforter.

Occasionally she poked a fresh twig into the fire which was an essential feature of any picnic. This action could arouse visible annoyance in my mother. Fires were sacrosanct, and when they were together my mother considered that the prerogative of tending the flame was hers. But for Nannie also the hearth was of great symbolic importance. Her father, a man who worked with iron, had presented each of his children with a poker when they went out into the world. Something ancient and atavistic in both Nannie and my mother responded to the sight of a circle of stones or a grate with a fire in it. This represented home, the centre and symbol of identity and influence, and each fiercely resented any tampering by the other with 'their' fires. At The Lodge, in drawing room or nursery, there was no doubting whose was the ownership of the fire. On picnics, however, the language of the flames plainly indicated the fine balance of tension that lay between my mother and her Nannie.

On these expeditions my mother was the cook. The small stove on which she fried sausages and Wattie's tomatoes, was a very dangerous gadget. Primed by my father it hissed fiercely and usually burst into flames once or twice before beginning to purr steadily and settle down ready for use. In summer we took a great basket of strawberries to eat on the banks of the Garpol or the River Ae. In those cold fresh waters we sometimes bathed, an exercise in sheer masochism requiring afterwards all the comfort of Nannie's towels and my mother's sausages.

Holidays were altogether another matter. In the early years there was no such thing as last minute improvisation. Planning was detailed and thorough. The whole house had to be shut up and put under dust sheets before we left. Where Nannie was concerned nothing went under a dust sheet that was not previously spotlessly cleaned, and ready for instant use on our return. Not for her the procrastinations of the indolent covering up a multitude of sins of omission in the hope that they might never come to light.

My parents took a house at the seaside and the entire household moved there. The day of departure, which started before dawn, was as carefully controlled as any army movement order could have made it. The maids left by train, as did an accumulation of assorted baggage, bed linen for everyone, prams, trunks, suitcases, hatboxes, golf clubs, spades, receptacles for sand. It cost £14 to send the luggage. In 1914 that had been Nannie's yearly salary.

It was to be hoped that the maids arrived before us. We, driving in a leisurely fashion in the Minerva, excited, almost beyond bearing, by remembered landmarks, were occasionally subject to bouts of car sickness. We wished desperately at the sight of a white horse, but were unable to maintain the essential silence until the second ingredient in the spell came into view to make our wishes come true and release us from it. We chanted rhymes about the magical properties of magpies, sniffed the salt tang of the Firth of Forth and listened to stirring tales of Scottish history told us by my mother. At last, catching sight of the great mound of Berwick Law rising out of the flat plain, with its whalebone jaws astride the summit, we knew that we were very nearly there.

My mother was a devoted bather. She loved the sea and believed in its curative properties. We learned to swim, reluctantly, under professional instruction at the swimming pool; but it is the enormous white towels that Nannie wrapped us in when we came out of the waves that I remember. She sat just outside a bathing hut, surrounded by all the adjuncts of a beach rescue service and an endless supply of those same towels. She was the guardian of normality, eyes alert for small disasters, prepared to restore us to calm and order if our holiday extravagances got out of hand. If my father scraped a finger while engaged as contractor for an expanding sandcastle, it was Nannie who produced first aid; if my mother lost a ring or a watch on the dunes – which happened frequently – it was Nannie who searched patiently until it was found; if we needed to be warmed up, or cooled down, given drinks, reprimanded for naughtiness or made to see that we were not after all being victimised, it was Nannie who succoured us with the known and respected nostrums of the nursery.

Once my mother made of Nannie a fellow conspirator when, crippled with fibrositis, she determined to defy express orders to the contrary and immerse herself in the sea. While Nannie kept watch, aware of her own physical frailty and agitated beyond measure at the prospect of trying to rescue her employer if anything went wrong, my mother clad in her husband's bathing suit subjected herself to the health-giving properties of salt water. She did not drown. The remedy worked, and only when improvement was noticeable did she tell my father what she had been doing while he taught his children golf.

Later, in less style in an Armstrong Siddeley, we went to Lossiemouth on the Moray Firth, where my father, alas, discovered the sovereign potential of Elgin Cream and my mother continued her love affair with the sea. The maids departed for their own holidays instead of coming on ours, and we roosted in rooms where the landlady cooked for us. Nannie, of course, came too, by now woven into the pattern of our family life in a way that hardly admitted of even temporary exclusion.

Yet we barely recognised our dependence on her. As we grew older she represented the nursery from which we wanted to escape. She ate with us the meals presented by our landlady, which my kind-hearted father could not bear to criticise. He hid his rice pudding in the earth under the potted fern and then praised its consistency – only to reap the reward of his good nature in a repeat performance the next day. Nannie came with us to CSSM services on the beach, where we entered sandcastle competitions and learned to sing choruses that stayed with us all our lives. To be able to 'Throw out the lifeline' with vocal abandon to the accompaniment of a wheezy portable organ and our father's enthusiastic support gave us all immense enjoyment. Nannie was there when we went to see the shifting Culbin Sands, and joined the combined picnics when we met our aunts and cousins. She knew all our relations and the intricate ramifications of our kin as well as we did – rather better sometimes, for my mother trusted her as a loyal and discreet confidante. Her position exempted her from the urge to communicate that, in times of stress, afflicted most of those attached by right of birth to the family grapevine.

We were no longer babies by the time we went to Lossiemouth, and while for my mother we were still within the safe orbit of her own world, for Nannie the springtime of proprietorship had already past. I too was beginning to be conscious that the balance of my personal world was changing. I had always been aware that I was different. In a household geared largely to male pursuits I was accustomed to accommodating my wishes to suit those of others. Indeed I hardly knew that I had wishes of my own. But now, in a special way, I began to perceive that I stood between Nannie and my mother and that sometimes this position required me to tread cautiously, and to watch my words and actions with care.

*   *   *

Shades of the prison house, the substance of boarding school, reached out to take possession of us when Robert was still very young. It was then that Nannie began to knit red stockings and I, now the proud sister of a schoolboy, needed to be dressed for the public occasions on which my presence at the functions of his establishment was required.

From the day that she had become responsible for a ten-day old bundle in a white shawl Nannie had made most of my clothes. As some pianists can play a piece by ear after hearing it only once, so she had the ability to recreate any model that was shown her. She could use patterns with flair and imagination, but such a prop was not essential to her art. As I grew older my mother loved to send for dresses 'on approval', even from shops as far away as London. She had an eye for pretty clothes and enjoyed spending money on them. My father, on the contrary, liked only those things that Nannie made for me. To him his daughter was special, and perhaps he felt that her uniqueness was emphasised if the things she wore had been created for her alone. So it sometimes happened that Nannie saw a dress which had arrived 'on appro', and then copied it in material and colour to suit my needs – while the original goods were quietly returned to the London store.

It was not only for me that Nannie sewed and knitted. When school loomed it was chiefly on my brothers' behalf that her knitting needles were occupied. At one period she kept them in thirty pairs of stockings, ten pairs each – four scarlet (the school colour), four tweed (for plus fours) and two tartan (for a kilt) – replaced, refooted and refurbished as they wore out. To these were added cable stitch sweaters, sports jerseys in appropriate colours, anything and everything that could be made out of wool.

Every time any of us moved out of the house we were a walking advertisement for Nannie's skills. My brothers' friends used to beg to be allowed to share in this bounty, especially the stockings. No one else we knew had access to such a wealth of beautiful garments; no other Nannie had the talents of ours. In a community where the hand-made was still valued above the shop-bought we were rightly envied.

Her fame as a seamstress was known outside The Lodge

garden. She won prizes at the local Agriculture and Flower Show, and constant requests were relayed through my mother for Nannie HR to fill a stall for Church sales of work, to design and cut out tiny cotton jackets for the Woman's Guild to make up for the mission field, or to shape the skirts and dresses that would eventually find their way to India and Africa. So, with exquisite artistry, Nannie dressed dolls and made beautiful baby clothes, crocheted squares and fashioned out of them exotic coloured blankets, knitted soft toys. Never a member of the Woman's Guild, never a part of the fellowship that built on her foundations, she was yet the essential element in maintaining the high standard of the goods that were packed in large cardboard boxes and despatched on a journey that would take them to lands and peoples many thousand miles removed from our nursery in Moffat.

Neither Nannie, nor my mother on her behalf, ever refused a request. Whatever twinges of envy she may have felt, my mother knew that her talents were not of the same order as Nannie's. In the latter she had a kind of possessive pride. For Nannie the exercise of her skills brought profound satisfaction, and perhaps recognition by a wider audience compensated her for our often casual acceptance of her many gifts.

However, she herself could show a cruel disregard for our feelings when it came to the old, well-worn and much loved among our possessions. Nothing was sacred; indeed nothing was truly ours. Jumble sales which we regarded as innocent amusements, would suddenly, after it was too late, be found to be the vehicle by which a precious jersey or other garment had been wrested from us. Missionary boxes needed clothes; Christmas charities wanted toys; children in need, whose parents appealed to my father, found themselves the recipients of what we considered our property. Permission was never asked. It was not for us to question decisions made by those in authority over us; but the wounds of affronted dignity, thwarted affection, autocratic dispossession, often went deep.

Alastair, deprived without warning at a moment of crisis of the cardboard box that made a stable for his horse and cart, shouted, 'I'll never forgive you, Nannie. I'll never forgive you.' For the moment he meant it. I felt as deeply as he did about my abducted belongings but, not being a fighter, I sulked. But equally, one day, when affected no doubt by prevailing fashions that we none of us thought ever touched her Nannie suggested cutting her abundant hair, Alastair cried out in alarm, 'Oh no no Nannie! You mustn't.' In a world in which we ourselves were constantly changing it was important to us that she remain the same.

★   ★   ★

The return of a schoolboy to our nursery in the holidays reinforced its importance, rather than diminishing it. Although we continued to walk with Nannie up to the Crows' Wood, a more daring element entered into our activities and brought us home to nursery tea dishevelled, dirty – and occasionally dented. To the accompaniment of much scorn and not a little pain I learned to play cricket. We fished in the burn behind our house, the triumph of catching a minnow obliterated by the torment of taking it off the hook. We guddled dangerously in the shadows under the overhanging bank. We dropped leaf and twig boats into the current above the bridge and rushed, breathless, across the road to watch for their emergence on the other side. We turned on the garden hose when Wattie was not looking, drenched each other and flooded the garage yard. We climbed the Gallow Hill with my father, braving with beating hearts the fields of cows, cutting ourselves sticks to switch at the undergrowth and repel any hanged man's ghost that might be lurking there. Now it was we who rowed a nervous Nannie in the Park boats, catching crabs and twirling helplessly among the indignant swans.

We began to bicycle recklessly around our house, in opposite directions to the great danger of our persons; or down the front lane – only to fling ourselves into the hedge at the bottom when speed and the prospect of imminent dissolution frightened us into instant abandonment. Once I rode through a new, and cherished, coral rhododendron bush of my father's and ruined it, angering my mother by seeking whole-hearted forgiveness from him before she or Nannie had a chance to mete out punishment.

Now on Sundays, after coming back from church, we had our lunch downstairs in the dining room. My father had a store of Biblical word games and quizzes which we enjoyed. We gave no thought to Nannie, eating in the nursery in solitary splendour – for the day of the nursery maid was long gone. For Nannie it was a foretaste of the time when we would have left her altogether; for us it was the threshold of a wider world.

When holidays ended and Robert departed we, who were left, bicycled round to a small school outside our back gate. It was kept by the widow of the man who had owned the newspaper shop. There were two cycles for the three of us. Laurence took Alastair on his back step, where he was in grave danger of being mauled by a pair of Pekinese dogs whose yapping fury we had to brave each morning. They belonged to elderly sisters related to 'bonnie Annie Laurie' and lived, unfortunately, over the hedge from our vegetable garden. No matter the weather, no matter the cunning with which we tried to unlock the gate and sneak our bicycles out of it, they were always there – prepared to leap at our ankles and draw blood from legs flung hastily over saddles. They hated us – as we hated them. I wondered if they reflected some sentiment of their mistresses that was never expressed to my mother over the delicate china and thin sandwiches of the elegant Laurie tea-table. But the Pekes had their territorial limits, from our back gate to twenty yards down the road. Once clear of this invisible boundary we could slacken our pace and yell rudely back at their quivering, growling, slobbering forms.

The only other hazard, of quite a different nature, lay in the possibility of a meeting with the Miss 'Bun-buns'. They were poor and elderly, living in part of a black stone house behind a grey stone wall and a row of lowering fir trees. There were three of them, spinster sisters from another age. Thin, tall, wearing long straight dark clothes, they got their name from the immense quantities of thick grey hair wound up in coils under their huge beehive hats. They were timid gentle women and we laughed at them; but something in the strangeness of their appearance made me always fear that one day a confrontation might have quite another outcome of an altogether more sinister kind.

For myself change came with sickening suddenness the day Laurence joined Robert at boarding school. He must have been nine: I was eleven and a half. There had been many preparations, shopping and packing, knitting and naming, an extra tuck box to be filled, special treats, Jean excelling herself with favourite dishes. It was an event looked forward to without trepidation, a start to an outside life of whose reality we had little idea. He wanted to go, and had a temperament which anticipated welcome – thus ensuring in some situations its opposite. I was adoring and proud.

Then the day came and he went, suddenly small and unprotected. Out of the blue I felt devastatingly desolated. I wept and wept and would not be comforted. An only girl among boys, I was used to being cherished, dependent, teased, guarded; it was the female role. But my instincts and my eyes told me otherwise – that it was the women who humoured and cared for the family, whose strength defended it, whose steadfastness built walls around it. For the first time, because he was younger and I had often championed his cause when trouble threatened, I found myself joining my mother and Nannie as a protector. In this situation the knowledge of my helplessness was more than my heart could bear. What Nannie felt, now that the second of her 'birds' had left the nest, it would never have occurred to me to ask.

She had been with us eleven years at this time. We had begun to outgrow her literally as well as metaphorically.

Whatever my father thought, she still looked forward to having other babies under her care. It was after all a hazard of her profession that infants grew up and Nannies became expendable. Nannie F was about to leave her family. Our Nannie had known from the beginning that we would leave her, and she us. She was perhaps better armoured against the inevitable time than was my mother, whose strong possessive instincts fought with her pride in the youthful achievements of her sons. When Alastair went away to school, and I also would be gone, a climax still a year or two in the future, then Nannie would seek another family and another job.

Meantime there was no lack of things to do. Almost without our noticing she had become a kind of major domo, a ready source of practical help, prepared to accept any responsibility, to listen to whatever those who came up to the nursery to see her wanted to say. Visiting aunts would enjoy retailing the family gossip, visiting cousins brought their clothes to be mended or ironed. In an indirect fashion my mother had come to rely on her more and more to assist in the smooth running of domestic affairs. Though Nannie admired my mother and began, often to the latter's irritation, to copy her taste in clothes and personal possessions, in her heart of hearts she considered her employer incompetent in matters of everyday household management.

It was in time of illness that Nannie's flair for good administration came to the fore.

Though, like fine weather, the prevailing climate of my childhood seems now to have been a healthy one, in fact both my mother and my father suffered considerably during the long winter months from bouts of illness – and from the anxiety that went with their constant concern for each other. My mother had trouble with her chest and caught bad colds. It was Nannie who supervised arrangements for the sickroom, beat up eggs in milk, and took over the housekeeping in her absence, My father's headaches often brought him upstairs to his small study when there were visitors in the drawing room. From there he would slip across to the nursery opposite, to have a cup of tea and one of her round wheaten scones with Nannie.

Once my mother came close to death. She developed erysipelas in an Edinburgh nursing home and her condition deteriorated rapidly until her life hung in the balance. When it seemed that all hope must be given up my father and the family doctor made the decision, against considerable opposition, to bring her home.

Nannie was instructed to get the master bedroom cleared and scrubbed. The great four poster was dismantled by the men from the mill and replaced by a narrow iron hospital bed. There were nurses to be catered for, fresh linen to be bought and sterilised; the house to be made ready to receive a dying woman.

With her usual efficiency Nannie dealt with the practical problems, calmed the agitated maids and issued instructions. Then she prepared us for our mother's arrival in circumstances very different from any we had known before.

At this point Nannie F's employer, an old family friend, arrived to offer help. He said that he would take the children away until the situation in their own home had resolved itself one way or the other. He was a commanding man, accustomed to having his own way and certain of the rightness of his judgments.

Nannie did not see the position in the same light as he did. My father had said nothing about removing the children, and in her own mind she was certain that the knowledge of their close presence might do more to bring my mother back from the shores of death than clean rooms and good nursing could ever accomplish. Drawing up her small frame, her mouth between its full cheeks closing in an obstinate line, she refused to let us go.

He was not accustomed to being thwarted, especially by a woman – and in a subordinate position at that. On both sides the emotional tension rose. They confronted each other; Nannie already overburdened and expecting the ambulance to arrive at any moment, Nannie F's employer, affronted by the rebuff to his genuine desire to help and pricked in his pride by his inability to bully our Nannie into the kind of submission he certainly expected from his own. She stood in his way, resolute to defend her children from the designs of any outsider, however great a friend, however well intentioned.

Eventually, with a bad grace, he went, but he left his car and chauffeur at the bottom of the lane, as a reminder to Nannie that she was taking on herself a responsibility he thought not hers to assume and a sign of his conviction that she would, given time, inevitably change her mind.

Two hours late the ambulance arrived, with my father following after it in his car. Twice on the road the little procession had had to stop because it was feared my mother was dead. Twice she was resuscitated and the journey to bring her home to die continued. When, frail but conscious, she was at last installed in her own room Nannie, in some trepidation, broached the subject of the car and chaffeur still sitting patiently at the foot of the lane. She passed on the offer to remove us from the scene.

'Certainly not', my father said. With triumph well concealed Nannie sent a messenger down the drive to deliver this definitive refusal.

Within a week the night nurse returned to Edinburgh and my mother was on the way to recovery.

★   ★   ★

In the summer term just after my thirteenth birthday I went away to boarding school. Beforehand my father's fussiness over the clothes his daughter wore had brought Nannie and my mother together in common exasperation.

Practically every item on the long clothing list was made by Nannie: ten blouses with eighty button holes, ten dresses with matching knickers, blue serge sports knickers with knicker linings, pyjamas. While Nannie sat at her machine working away at the navy blue cotton dresses that were required, my mother embroidered tiny coloured motifs on the collars. Over them both my father hovered anxiously, commenting, testing, even protesting when he felt that some extra flourish of decoration might make me conspicuous. There was no experience of girls in boarding school to guide them, but he remembered from his own schooldays the desperate need of every new boy to appear exactly like his fellows. In the end my mother ejected him from the nursery, telling him firmly to leave such decisions to those who knew how to deal with them.

His instinct, however, was right – though misdirected. I was no longer the fat baby who had tumbled down the stairs but a lanky overgrown plain shy girl, who sometimes heard the word skinny being bandied about. To save my feelings if stick-like arms were exposed to the gaze of unkindly disposed contemporaries, all summer frocks were made with long sleeves.

All that endless term it seemed to me to be a major catastrophe. Not only did such singularity attract a good deal of often ribald attention, it revealed to me my own immense inadequacy. Of course I should have cut them off, as was so often urged on me, but I had not the courage. It was not Nannie's bewilderment and hurt at the destruction of her work that I feared, it was my mother's.

Boarding school was a turning point in my life, much anticipated, which lamentably failed to come up to expectations. For Nannie the massive involvement in preliminary preparations may even have resulted in a certain measure of relief when the day at last came that she was left for a short while longer with only one inhabitant for the nursery. Once Alastair flew the nest there was a tacit understanding that Nannie's time with us would come to an end. Nannie, wiser than we were, lived with the knowledge that there were other nurseries waiting for her skills. She had launched us on the next stage of life and we were considered to do her credit. There was no hurry to make the change but, though the very mention of fresh household arrangements upset my father,

her eyes and ears were already tuned to the market place.

Then my father died.

It was a bad winter, with a great deal of influenza about. He took ill on Christmas Day, but struggled to conceal it until the holidays were over. Towards the end of January, suddenly, he died.

In the orbit of this tragedy my mother and Nannie, who had shared the last fourteen years of family life and formed a protective ring about my father, drew closer together. In her shock and confusion, and under the necessity of making a thousand and one different arrangements, my mother turned to Nannie rather than to friends and relatives. It was Nannie whose steady common sense helped to resolve the problems that beset us all. It was Nannie to whom the maids turned, who dealt with callers, made me a mauve velvet dress to take back to school. For my mother, upright, self-controlled, fiercely protective of her children, Nannie was perhaps the only person at that moment on whose loyalty she felt she could completely rely. At the funeral my mother's unmarried sisters assured her that one of them could always come to stay if wanted. My mother simply said, 'No. I've got Nannie. We've been through it all together.'

My mother took me back to school. It was a winter of bad snow and on the return journey the train from the south was unconscionably delayed. When, at three in the morning, it at last drew in to Beattock Station it was Nannie, with a taxi, who was sharing an orange juice with the porter in his tiny room – all other friends having fallen by the wayside when the full extent of the sacrifice required became apparent.

Because a letter had miscarried Nannie was alone in the house when a man arrived from Glasgow to make an inventory for probate. Wattie, who had found him on the front path, brought him to her with the admonition, 'Nurse – don't you let him in'. Nannie too was apprehensive. He was a stranger, though he seemed presentable enough.

She allowed him into the house, with Wattie to keep an eye on him and strict instructions that he was to make notes of everything he did for my mother to see when she came back next day. Then she put on her hat and hurried down to the village to see the bank manager. Asking for a private word, she explained the situation and begged him to contact my mother's man of affairs in Glasgow to find out if the visitor was genuine.

On the telephone the man of affairs, who did not know her, confirmed the stranger's credentials but queried Nannie's trustworthiness. Nobody in Moffat would have hesitated to reassure him on this point and the bank manager did so. Nannie, who had heard this exchange, then hurried home to keep an eye on things.

In fact it was probable that she knew better than my mother what was what. She had an elephant's memory for the contents of attics and cupboards, the things put away in boxes, the household goods disposed of on shelves. She knew that it was usual for her bedroom suite to belong to a bride and that my mother's had been made for her – so she claimed it firmly as her mistress's. By mistake, and it afterwards worried her meticulous and honest soul, she swore that a dark cupboard in the drawing room passage had nothing in it, not realising that the one valuable china service concealed there had never been returned to the bank after the Christmas festivities.

My father had absolute confidence in Nannie's judgment. He had often said to her, 'You won't leave us Nannie, will you?'; and latterly, with premonition, 'You won't leave her Nannie?' It was a wish that was to bring much pain.

Moffat from Ballplay Road

AUTUMN

After my father died my mother asked Nannie if she would put aside any plans she might have been making and stay with us for another year. There was no question of such a request being refused. It echoed my father's own wishes, now powerfully reinforced by his death. So when we came back for the holidays Nannie was there as usual, and we took it for granted that she should be.

Though we must have known that our infancy was ended, and no doubt accepted this development with equanimity, it was nevertheless a very great shock to come home from school and find the nursery gone.

This beautiful room, which when we first moved into The

Lodge my mother's friends had thought too good for us, now became the family sitting room.

The transformation was to be a surprise and my mother, who had spared no effort to make it as comfortable and as welcoming as possible, must have been taken aback and hurt at the reception given to her carefully planned unveiling of this well-kept secret. Living between two women of strong personality, whose open expressions of dissent or anger with each other may have been therapeutic for them but had become painful for me, I had learned to keep much of what I thought to myself. But it cannot have been possible to control the expression of appalled disbelief on my face when the nursery door was first opened, or interpret my lukewarm answers to eager questions as anything but disapproval.

Inside I was enraged. Without consultation, taking it for granted that our wishes paralleled her own, my mother had suddenly bereft us of our childhood. The core of the familiar comforts of home had been removed without warning. Nothing was where it should have been, not even Nannie. Where were my books, my paints, dolls not yet quite discarded, the old toy box? Where was the old-fashioned fireside guard on which we sat, the ping-pong table – replaced by the piano? This room, which had been our kingdom, was now to be shared with other people, and already the stamp of the invader had been set upon it.

Of course, in time, we accepted the alteration. The room in its new guise gradually reached out and claimed us. But for Nannie it put the seal on a fundamental shift in her position, and though I remember my own reaction as being a purely selfish one I cannot help feeling that what had happened to Nannie also played a part in it.

Nannie had been displaced. As so often, a change long maturing unnoticed and unforeseen sprang ready-made out of the shadows and redirected the currents of our life. A small room across the landing, the parlour which my father had used as a study, had been turned into what was to become known as 'Nannie's room'. Both for her and for ourselves

72

the nomenclature made plain a mutation in our relationships. We no longer rushed in as of right. We did not any more share a territory with her distinct from that of the other inmates of the house. We had moved on, to meals in the dining room, to full citizenship in every part of our home.

But Nannie's status had diminished. For a long while there had been no undernurse and we took up the trays of food which she ate alone. The furniture and decoration in her new room were our family's – perhaps she liked it that way, but there had been little transfer of the thought and care which went to make the old nursery suitable for us. The common ground that had once supported us was beginning to dissolve; her link with us now that authority had gone relied on affection and goodwill. Only in the curious little square connecting room, known as the toy room, that lay between our old nursery and Nannie's new abode, with doors to each, housing the toy box, a huggermugger of books and magazines – *Tiger Tim*, the *Boys' Own Paper* and the *Children's Newspaper* – games and puzzles, Nannie's ironing board and sewing machine, her boxes of buttons and balls of wool, in this repository of the accumulated clutter of a shared past our lives were still inextricably intermixed.

Mine was joined in another way that did not always give me satisfaction. Alastair had long moved out of the night nursery to a room of his own and Nannie had the bedroom to herself. But it remained approachable only through mine and this lack of privacy irked me greatly. I had no fellow feeling for Nannie trapped in a like situation where she must often have been aware of my irritated adolescent eyes following her progress through my room with a hostility I seldom felt there was any need to disguise. I took it badly that I could never shut my door and feel safe from intrusion, though Nannie, perhaps more conscious of my feelings than I gave her credit for, was scrupulous in her passages to and fro to ignore my petulant presence. She went to bed much earlier than I and was safely shut away when my turn came, but the knowledge of her occupancy at such close quarters inhibited the use that I might have made of my solitutde. Visions of poultices and epicacuhana sugar lumps, of being admonished and tucked in, exhorted to get on with my dressing and to keep my drawers tidy, haunted me long after it had been tacitly accepted that I was capable at least of making token gestures towards looking after myself.

Somehow the twelve months that my mother had requested stretched on and on. In the years that followed, while we grew up and began to test ourselves against the greater world, Nannie was always present when we returned, her arms outstretched, a welcoming smile on her face as she embraced us.

But an element of uneasiness had entered into her relationship with my mother which I, increasingly essential to their equilibrium, did my best to ignore. I had problems enough of my own. For long periods the house was empty of children. The living focus of much that Nannie continued to do, sewing, attaching Cash's name-tapes to every conceivable article, filling tuck boxes, knitting, mending, patching, was necessarily absent. And when present we were no longer dependent on her, and often indifferent to her need of us in concern for our mother's greater need.

As the first year after my father's death drew to an end, Nannie began to get restless and unhappy, uncertain of where her future lay, drawn to stay, pulled to go. She waited for my mother to tell her that the time had come to part and my mother, whose dependence grew while ours diminished, could not bring herself to do so.

There are some close relationships in life into which friendship does not enter – and because of this they are the more difficult to preserve when times change. Such was the tie between my mother and Nannie, which in spite of everything was to prove indissoluble. The bonds that held them together were loyalty, respect and a joint experience. The love that bound them was love of us – and of my father's memory. Had they parted those components would have kept them close. From a distance common memories of happiness and tragedy, and of all the intimacies of our childhood which they alone now shared, would have drawn them back frequently to the warmth of each other's company.

But temperament and circumstances more often choose our course for us than logic, or even desire. Though life could be difficult and there were times when each thought the other unreasonable, somehow the decision to separate was never taken. Held by the past, there seemed no way of crossing old boundaries to an acceptance of fresh terms, nor to assuage the guilt which tinged the contemplation of separation with betrayal.

Nevertheless, though shadowed by friction and intermittently haunted by a fear of war, those next years were happy ones.

Jean had left to be married before my father died. Now Lucy, who had taken over the kitchen, went to nurse her own mother. Urged to make financial savings, it seemed natural to my mother to turn to Nannie.

That Nannie should be in the kitchen was understood to be a temporary situation, and though it was to last many years it somehow never seemed to assume an air of permanency. She had come down, both literally and figuratively, from her immaculate airy nursery to work in a semi-basement with a cold stone floor; but she was once again at the centre of the household, and it was from 'Nannie's room' that she held the reins.

Downstairs physical conditions were very different. Although there was a series of young women to help, cooking on a solid fuel range with flues to be kept clean, using heavy cast iron pots, being responsible for much of the scrubbing and scouring which went with kitchen work and overseeing the 'girl', occasionally tried both body and temper. Being the perfectionist she was, Nannie was no more content to accept lower standards below stairs than she had been above.

Not long after my father's death, Nannie's own father

died. He was sixty-six and for some time his health had been deteriorating. It must have been another disorientating blow for Nannie who had always been fond of him. After the funeral she brought her mother to Moffat to stay in our home for a while and enjoy the peace of Wattie's garden.

We were all away at school now, my brothers in Edinburgh and I in England. For long periods of time my mother and Nannie were alone together. When we came back for the holidays we had lives of our own to lead which rarely included Nannie. But she still worked for us, came on our picnics, was always in demand when things were mislaid, we had got into a scrape or needed a sympathetic uncritical ear.

She too needed a listener – as did my mother. Though to outsiders they presented a united front, especially when they suspected that we might be being seduced from our primary allegiance, increasingly there were times when they wanted to grumble about each other. In this situation I was the natural confidante, the consultant to whom both turned. I knew that the first few days after each return would be spent exploring delicately how the land lay between Nannie and my mother.

When we went away again the need for companionship once more drew them together.

If there was reason to go to Glasgow or Edinburgh, to visit relatives, to shop, or to my brothers' school for matches or exeats, Nannie sat beside my mother on the long drive through the hills. In summer the road from Moffat to Edinburgh, up the slow climb to the rim of the Beef Tub past the cemetery where my father lay, was a pleasant one. Larks sang above the open rolling hillsides that crowned the Tub, where the three rivers Annan, Tweed and Clyde rose among the harebells and ling. The black-faced sheep that cropped the short tussocky grass on the unfenced moorland had priority over the motorist, who was constantly admonished by notices to be careful and beware. On fine days the sheep lay on the road and motor cars drove round them. Once one leaped straight over a dyke on to our bonnet. In late summer the hilltops were purple and pink and the bracken turned golden. Nannie sat beside my mother, content to be silent but perfectly understanding half-voiced observations, ready to add her quota to family reminiscence with an ear well-tuned to the nuances of query or statement.

But in winter this road could present a very different aspect. Then there was significance in the squat memorial, set in the wastes just beyond the lip of Moffat valley, which commemorated the valiant deed, in February 1831, of the driver and guard of the mail coach who abandoned their horses and vehicle in a heavy snow storm to try to get the mail through from Moffat to Edinburgh on foot – and died in the attempt.

Then on the return journey there could be a damp clinging fog on the Broughton marshland and, as the car climbed steadily up out of the lowlands, driving rain or sleet or heavy wet snow. Windscreen wipers clogged up; all sense of direction evaporated as a drifting white curtain reflected back the headlights or thick mist parted with ghostly smoothness to reveal a bare stunted hangman's tree that had no business to be there. The road surface slid away beneath the tyres and in all the acres of the moors no single other human being seemed to have been left alive.

On such nights as these strong men had been known to shrink from this journey, preferring the comfort of a hotel at one end or their own beds at the other. But for my mother no weather was ever too bad. She was an intrepid driver; she was also determined never to fail her sons. Beside her, displaying the most perfect confidence in her skills, Nannie sat calmly through the worst of blizzards.

Once, in thick snow, the car skidded out of control across the highway, up a grass bank, to end up back on the road facing in the direction it had come. Both women remained cool, Nannie full of admiration for my mother's handling of the motor in this emergency. Only when they clambered out to assess the damage did she find her legs trembling. Then they got in again and continued the journey home, and it was some time before either revealed to anyone that they had come close to serious injury. So another link was added to the chain that bound them.

When Nannie went into hospital for a major operation my mother missed her sorely, both as worker and companion. Nannie, who had always been the carer, lying in a hospital bed with a fearful unspoken query over it, seemed to have become involved in some monstrous reversal of the normal course of life. She returned to The Lodge much sooner than she should, chafed by convalescent dependence on her relatives, urged by my mother to come back to what was in effect her home – with the incentive of a promise of additional help.

As the years went on and menace lurked increasingly behind the headlines, I often sought the sanctuary of Nannie's room to escape from news bulletins on the wireless. Then to watch Nannie's sewing machine whirring peaceably through layers of material or listen to her knitting needles clicking round yet another pair of stockings and chat in a desultory fashion about the trivia of our shared lives held at bay for a short while the stealthy, unacknowledged, dread approach of war.

Perhaps of all of us in those times of growing up it was Alastair, the youngest, whose relationship with Nannie was the easiest, the most open and unabashed. The rest of us knew that we must be careful not to upset the balance between my mother and Nannie, and this consciousness of an equilibrium to be preserved inhibited us in our outward dealings with the latter. We did not want to ruffle my mother; and, for entirely selfish reasons, we did not want Nannie to fulfil the threats she sometimes made and desert us. Once she told me that she had the offer of a job in China – an impossible and romantic setting in which I found it difficult to place the Nannie I knew. I wondered occasionally if she invented those offers of employment to retune our awareness of her value to us. But while she remained with my mother it might be possible for me to leave.

In 1938, after university, Robert left for East Africa and the

Colonial Service. He went fully equipped with household goods, hardware, glass and china bought by my mother in Woolworths – no single item over sixpence; and linen – some of it made, all of it named, by Nannie. We saw him off with pride to join others of our kin who were serving overseas. But also with the knowledge that this was a parting with greater implications for change than any that had gone before. He was to be a married man and a father before we saw him again.

★   ★   ★

Very early in my life I had determined to go to Art College. I was accepted by Edinburgh. My mother and Nannie followed me there.

It was a difficult moment. The rational arguments for taking a house in the city for the winter were sensible and I found it impossible to articulate the feelings that made such a decision an unhappy one for me. There were still two brothers younger than myself at school in Edinburgh. Living there those long winter drives could be avoided. Now that I had returned from boarding school, my mother's chief thought was that I had come home and the years when she had been so much alone were ended. No doubt she had other reasons that she did not mention. I think now that she was afraid for me, let loose among artists; and, though we tried not to believe it, the heaviness that lay day and night, unrelieved, on our hearts told us that war was not far off. She remembered another war and she wanted us to be together when this one came.

But for my part, though I had been away at school, the end of this exile did not indicate to me a coming home, but rather freedom to explore an individual way of life. I knew myself to be susceptible to the smallest obligations of love or duty, by nature a keeper of other people's rules, the conciliator in the midst of others' controversies. Now, at last, I would be able to find out what talents I possessed and to exercise them in surroundings where the only purposes I need pursue were my own.

It was not yet to be.

It was a bad winter, full of gloom and foreboding, and the sitting room in the rented house had a black ceiling. January was the month in which my father had died. At this time my mother's physical health had always been at its lowest, now her spirit too found the days hard to live through.

Change of scene, however, did not alter Nannie's perennial occupations. She fed us and looked after us, and continued to make me dresses on slippery Victorian tables. But thrown together, in much closer quarters than usual, their individual talents and concerns in the Moffat community cut off from them, she and my mother turned the full focus of their attention on me.

Alas for the long evenings drinking coffee and discussing Life and Art that I had so happily envisaged. Time had not yet become the hoped for fluid entity dependent on no one's wishes but my own. In the evenings we three sat together, nerve ends tingling, antennae alert to intercept unspoken messages, to head off questions that might result in confrontation. On the table the small wireless set remained silent, until the strain of ignorance became too much and one of us had the courage to turn on the news.

I seethed with frustrations that could not be expressed, imagining my friends engaged in infinitely enticing Bohemian orgies – of the mildest and most innocuous kind. One of them, at least, had a home in Edinburgh and was almost certainly sitting, as I was, with her parents – but that did not occur to me. On Friday nights she and I and one other went together to the cinema. But even then I regretted the dawdling easy fellowship afterwards in which I imagined we might have indulged – if we had been able to find a coffee bar open – but which my conscience, demanding an early return home, never let me contemplate.

No doubt my mother too found those long evenings joyless. She had her daughter by her, but something in her –

which she fought to control – resented the close contact in which she must share her with Nannie. And Nannie, sitting peacefully knitting or sewing, finding no need to speak, going early to bed, knowing probably better than we did ourselves all that lay behind the anguish of tormented love that kept us silent, cannot have been without her own fears and frustrations to add to the current of subterranean feeling that swirled about that black ceilinged room. By a curious coincidence the most brilliant young painter in my year was a relation of Nannie's, a fact neither he nor I ever referred to. Indeed he may have been unaware that the connection existed. His presence, however, reinforced my theory that there was a strain of genius in Nannie's family that had somehow by-passed our own.

But all winters end, and spring at last broke through. In the Easter holidays we went back to Moffat and when summer term began I found a room in a hostel. It was not yet the perfect freedom that I dreamed of, but it was halfway there, and by contrast the weekends at home, with Nannie's excellent food, were relaxed and enjoyable. I had given my mother a Siamese cat, a nervous elegant beast which rushed hysterically up and down curtains causing Nannie to curse the dratted creature under her breath. Shortly after it died in a convulsive fit.

It was a beautiful summer in 1939. We prepared for war – and could not believe it possible. Gas masks were issued and fitted by our policeman, leaving his bicycle at the wee gate and loitering up the path swinging the cardboard boxes, as though it were a visit of no particular significance. We never thought what such a demonstration must have done to Wattie, who sat in the greenhouse nursing lungs that had already suffered from this very evil and no doubt remembering another war.

In differing ways the village got ready. We watched each other limbering up with fear, amusement or scorn. Some began to lay in stores secretly – to be almost immediately exposed by rumour. It was already known who the potential hoarders were. Some dug trenches in unlikely places – it was a relief to criticise and air our own wisdom, though in truth we none of us had the least idea where, or how, or even why we should do these things. Men got together and talked of defending their families and homes. We all had the notion that the sky would be filled with German parachutists shortly after war was declared.

Once, driving back from Edinburgh, the sky over the Beef Tub turned steel grey, imparting an unstable eeriness to the landscape beneath it. Over all blazed a bright sapphire blue sun. When we reached it Moffat was preparing for the end of the world. Nannie was calm, but making arrangements – as was my mother. In a curious way the end of the world was in our house an everyday preoccupation. In the 1930s there were many groups who not only believed that it was coming but could even put a date to it, and my father had been interested in these things. I had lived already through at least one such certainty, going apprehensively to bed one night and waking up next morning quite surprised to find the witching hour of midnight passed and Nannie still sleeping quietly next door. The blue sun turned out to be caused by dust from a gigantic forest fire in the United States – and one more deadline disappeared into history, remembered only by the postman who made jokes reversing the old saying 'once in a blue moon'. But in 1939 an altogether more tangible threat hung over us, Armageddon itself, and I felt a good deal less confident of surviving it.

The grocer's shop at the corner of Well Street was a hot-bed of misinformation, with Duncan Mundell whispering urgently over the counter to favoured customers. Some people were said to have already built impregnable air raid shelters inside their own houses and to be preparing to retire there leaving the rest of us to cope as best we could. We suspected that this might be foresight – and maintained that it was selfish cowardice. A number of lads went off to Dumfries and enlisted, an action that seemed in specific instances astonishingly bold. One of the boys who had driven the milkcart returned to his home changed out of all recognition by a uniform – even a sloppy battledress. Women spoke soberly of practical matters and joined the Women's Voluntary Service (WVS). Their uniform was green, an unlucky colour; for the superstitious a real sacrifice was involved.

Alastair, on his first motorbike, rushed about the country-side seeking for news; Laurence, about to go to university, sank into silence while he wondered how he could convince my mother that it would be better for him to join up and considered what such a step into action would entail. She herself made lethal arrangements to prevent my falling into the hands of invading Huns. When, much later, I learned this, I was insulted beyond measure that she had not thought me capable of independent judgment or spirit. Nannie, quietly and without fuss, contrived blackout screens for all the windows and discreet plans to keep the household going whatever emergencies might arise. She had learned from the boys the arts of carpentry, and added mending fuses and unblocking drains to her armoury. When the time came she was to have a magical touch with ration books.

Nannie's war, in fact, began a good deal earlier than that of many other people.

On Saturday 2 September 1939 my mother took us all to Dumfries and we sat through two different film programmes, consecutively, in two different cinemas. Such indulgence was unknown. It confirmed our knowledge that the situation was desperate. At least in darkness we could come to terms, each in our own way, with our fears and tensions. The next morning, as we were getting ready for church, the siren went and a lone aircraft droned overhead. The sun was shining splendidly when we heard we were at war.

It had been known for some time that Moffat was a safe area and would be expected to take evacuees from Glasgow. A tentative survey had already been made by billeting officers. These were plans, like so many others, whose reality did not impinge until the day the town heard that a trainload of mothers and children was arriving from the Gorbals to seek our hospitality. Then indeed the community faced invasion for the first time, in a manner very far removed from the romantic, if fearful, inventions of the preceding weeks.

They came heralded by myth and rumour – and lived up to the worst fears that these had outlined. The Gorbals cast its shadow before it. 'They don't know what to do with a bath. They keep coals in it'. 'They'll be infested – nits, you know; fleas I shouldn't wonder'. 'A lot o' Glesca' keelies!' For both sides a rain of bombs would have made the situation easier, but the countryside lay basking in warm autumn sunshine and the city remained undisturbed. Two or three hundred exhausted, bedraggled, bewildered children clutching brown paper parcels or broken suitcases, with gas mask boxes and large luggage labels round their necks, staggered off the train and straggled under escort up the High Street to the Academy. Laurence, among others, supplied a ferry service for a number of pregnant mothers who came with them: Alastair became a motor cycle messenger. They were both exhilarated by action. At home Nannie, girded mentally to meet this crisis, grimly prepared physically for these un-wanted guests.

Arrangements for their reception at the school were full of goodwill – but primitive. Here were small human beings, most of whom had never been out of their own city street before, suddenly wrested from the familiar life of home and dumped down in a foreign country. They hardly knew why they had come and most of them were already homesick. The neat lists that had been made out in the last days of peace had taken no account of families who refused to be separated. There were large numbers who, to respectable country eyes, resembled nothing so much as ragamuffins, tinkers, tramps – for all their mothers had tried desperately to send them in their best clothes. Disorientation and a tediously slow train journey had counteracted last minute instructions. Most of us hardly understood what they were saying.

On the other hand promises made in the village when illusions still held sway evaporated in the face of reality, and were retracted without shame. Children anticipating a welcome knew themselves to be rejected when returned without compunction to the collecting point like unwanted goods sent out on approval. Many hitherto unacknowledged relations had suddenly pre-empted a number of Moffat spare rooms. On all sides tempers frayed and good intentions began to evaporate.

Quite late in the afternoon my mother and I brought home a family of seven, a mother with three children and three young relatives, and presented them to Nannie. I do not know how many the billeting officer had been told The Lodge could cope with, but at the Academy it had become clear as the day wore on that responsibility for her nieces and nephews was going to make it impossible for this woman to agree to the separation of her brood. Ours was the obvious home to take them all.

It was by no means an easy situation and the brunt of it fell on Nannie. My mother was frequently out, involved in village plans to meet the first arrival of troops. My brothers and I, preoccupied with our own responses to the war, frittered around the periphery. It was Nannie who had to organise beds and meals – discovering that much of her highly prized food was viewed with grave suspicion by these denizens from another world who wanted only fish and chips. It was Nannie who saw that all the children were scrubbed and went through their hair with a toothcomb; then doused the offending heads in a vinegar solution and wrapped them up in old towels. It was Nannie who eyed askance the meagre store of clothes in the misshapen suitcase and did her best to fill the gaps with hoarded garments from our younger days. It was Nannie who attempted to impose on this very different material something of the manners and discipline that had been our lot. It was Nannie who coped with a distraught mother, who had left provisions for her husband and when no air raids materialised did not know how he to was going to manage unless she returned to him.

The war was not old enough for traditional distinctions to have become blurred. My mother and Nannie still kept to their separate rooms. The evacuees were pushed unhappily into the interstices of our family home. They slept in the maids' rooms and ate in the kitchen. They were scrubbed in the deep old-fashioned bath in the top landing scullery. Accustomed to close communal living, they rattled about in our house like the contents of a nest of displaced mice. The adults on both sides tried to come to an accommodation; as the sense of urgency faded, on both sides they failed.

In the village old myths were replaced by new over the grocer's counter or in the kitchen of the newly-opened canteen opposite the Provost's shoeshop. Wherever small groups of Glasgow women got together to discuss the attitudes and arrangements of their hosts, homesickness was reinforced. Gradually, as no bombs materialised out of the heavens and the post brought an occasional angry note from an abandoned male, one or two women began to return home. A trickle of mothers travelled from Glasgow to reclaim children – who had sometimes just begun to settle down and enjoy themselves. It was not long before the mother in our family went back to look after her man taking her youngest with her. She felt, and who was to blame her, that she would rather face whatever the future brought in her own home among her neighbours than among strangers in an alien environment. Presently she sent for the other children too. The sense of failure was outweighed by the feeling of relief.

Nannie was to have two more waves of evacuees to deal with before the war settled into its long slow grind. When the bombs at last fell on Clydebank a fresh batch of children arrived. This time everyone was better prepared and they came without their mothers – which was generally agreed to be a good thing.

Nannie had only two in her charge, a red-headed brother and sister. They clung to each other terrified, answering questions in a breathy whisper and staring at Nannie as though she were a female ogre. She was brisk and kindly, but they found the actions she insisted upon – like having a bath – incomprehensible and her authority intimidating. More concerned with the effect of their natural habits on the cleanliness and order of our home than with any attempt to understand their lonely fears, she and my mother agreed that they should have the bedroom in which Jean, the cook, had slept. It was across the passage from the kitchen, at night remote from the rest of the house and its inhabitants. Clutched in each other's arms, urban babes in the wood, they lay awake shivering. It may well have been the first time that they had slept alone in a bed.

When my mother went to look at them, before herself going upstairs, she found them wide-eyed and staring. On being pressed they revealed that they were 'feart o' the birrds'. The silence of the long evenings, broken by sudden raucous flurries as the crows indulged in a last communal outing before settling down and smaller birds cheeped drowsily in the bushes, sounded infinitely more menacing to their town-bred ears than the clatter of tramcars, the brawling of neighbours or alcoholic ramblings in the close mouth.

Night after night they wet their beds. Morning after morning Nannie, to her exasperation, had to change the bedding, rinse the rubber sheeting, put the mattress out to air, wash their night clothes and find yet more ancient cloths for them to lie on. Even when the birds had ceased to frighten them and they had stopped feeling that they had been forcibly kidnapped by those who wished them ill, their beds remained soaking. The fact was that they were without the courage to get up in the darkness, to find their way along the stone passage to the toilet behind the wash-house, and preferred to suffer the discomfort of a clammy couch and the pursed lips of Nannie in the morning. At the time she was not pleased, though later she conceded that it was not surprising that they 'just did it in their beds'. In due time they returned to Glasgow. When they left bed and bedding had to be burnt.

Then, as a result of fresh alarms and an increase in urban bombing, Nannie got three brothers, sons of a widow. They too viewed with alarm the bracing initial exercises with which Nannie greeted them. When she discovered that they slept in the same clothes that they wore all day she went through secret boxes and cupboards of her own and presented each of them with an old viyella shirt. Then she explained that, after their baths, they could keep on their vests if they wished with the viyella shirts on top. In this way their own clothes would remain decent to wear during the day. The first night she went up to see that all was well they were sitting up in bed fully dressed under the viyella shirts.

Gradually, however, they relaxed their fierce possessiveness. Their mother was a woman of courage and character, who saw this disruption of normal life as an opportunity for her sons. She insisted on having their washing sent to her weekly. It came back laundered, patched and darned in a way that roused even Nannie's demanding admiration. She visited them and was appreciative of the chance that lay before them. In the peaceful surroundings of Moffat Academy they did well at school. They slept in the spare room, rather than in banishment beside the kitchen. They became interested in country pursuits and stayed on in Moffat, where more suitable long-term accommodation than The Lodge was eventually found for them. With the patina of Nannie's handiwork upon them they were launched into a new future.

In those first years there were other temporary residents of our home in need of Nannie's ministrations. In 1940 a tall handsome man in uniform, with a ravaged face, came up the path from the wee gate past the laburnum tree and rang our doorbell. With great courtesy, in halting English, he asked whether we had room to billet a Polish officer. Of course there was room, but it is not certain if my mother, by now very conscious of the strains and tensions of sharing her house, would have been easily persuaded if Laurence, at that moment at home, had not been determined that we should

Butcher's shop, formerly the gaol, Moffat

take the stranger in – especially when he discovered that it was for himself that the officer on the doorstep was seeking shelter.

The Poles took Moffat by storm and many hearts were lost, some permanently. Whatever the horrors that they had survived it was still in their nature to be gallant and romantic; after long months of disillusioning flatness here at last were soldiers who came from scenes of battle and had fought the enemy. A little later there might have been a more perceptive understanding of what had happened to them. At this moment, in a small town which as yet knew nothing of the pains and terrors of war, they must often have found the disjunction between their old life and their new hard to believe, sometimes the stuff of nightmare.

Through the voice of the Pole, who for a short time shared our home, once we caught a glimpse of hell and failed to recognise it for what it truly was.

He slept in the spare room, a man of great courtesy and melancholy charm. Whether he kissed Nannie's hand is not certain, but he treated my mother like a Queen. In his personal habits he was meticulous, perhaps a little more so than the sober Scottish household into which he had stepped could easily accept for there was a moment of stunned disbelief when it was discovered that he used scent. He refused to let Nannie sew on a button for him because it came off his pants, asking instead that she lend him needle and thread.

He ate in a mess, but in the evenings he would sit, brooding, on the opposite side of the fire from my mother. He was a Count, Captain in a Cavalry Regiment, whose estates, on which he thought his wife and children still lived, were now behind the line occupied by Russian troops. Suddenly, when answering my mother's questions about his family in broken English, he burst out, with a display of passion quite alien to our upbringing; 'Aiii! It is a cat-as-troff.'

It was as though a bomb had exploded in the quiet room. For an instant the disparity between his life and ours was savagely made plain. Yet, in the months to come, when we thought of him, what we remembered was his mispronounciation, the extraordinary sound he made of the word catastrophe.

By the time the Commandos came in 1941 both my brothers were on their way to the war, Laurence to end up in the Army in India, Alastair in the Royal Air Force. I had made an ill-starred attempt to be a nurse, but had developed a strong aversion to the treatment meted out to the female staff by young male doctors and, more seriously, an inability to remain upright when witnessing even the mildest injection – far less administering one myself. In a vacuum I returned to College to finish my diploma and was then to join the Church of Scotland's Huts and Canteens where caring took a less squeamish shape and where I was discomfited to find that, in official Service eyes, I was an OD – Other Denomination – co-existing with Baptists, Methodists, Quakers and anyone else who did not happen to be C of E. The exigencies of the heating situation had at last brought my mother and Nannie together on either side of the sitting room fire.

For a few months Moffat was the base for a troop belonging to No 2 Commando. It was not long since those units had been formed and we all knew that their function was to break out of embattled Britain, harrying and harassing the enemy on territory other than our own. By now the village was no stranger to sorrow. Telegrams had ceased to be objects received with pleasurable anticipation. In the Post Office Miss Rennie occasionally betrayed foreknowledge of private tragedy. Through her hands came the official announcements of death and wounds, the communications from prisoner-of-war camps.

Everything seemed to have gone wrong and we felt ourselves to be without friends. The threat of airborne invasion was always present. When they returned from patrols on the surrounding hills reports from some of the nervier Home Guards of strange appearances in the night sky did nothing to soothe prevailing jitters. Rumours of nuns with boots were rife. My mother chased a suspicious stranger up the High Street convinced that he was a spy. In this embattled, apprehensive atmosphere the Commandos gave us reassurance and promised offensive action to counter our defensive fears. We knew the risks they would eventually face as well as they did, and while they were in the village we hoped that they would never go; but all the same their jaunty acceptance of an aggressive future lifted our spirits.

They were privileged soldiers. None who followed them were billeted in private houses as they were. There was no time for the spit and polish or the household chores that most regiments took for granted, every available moment was to be spent on training. The morning they arrived their Captain, in battle dress, appeared on the doorstep of The Lodge requesting accommodation for two of his men. 'I'll see you get the Sergeants', he said, glancing round with approval – and the flattery was not without effect.

A short while later Bill and Peter, and their kit, were delivered to the door.

Though in every way different, they were friends. Bill was Scottish from near Glasgow, large, dark and dour – until his outer reserve was penetrated; Peter, from London, was of medium height and very fair, with a small corn-coloured moustache. He had panache and an easy way with him. He endeared himself to Nannie by stressing that the Captain had chosen them himself, and told them that they were going to a very special house. No apprehensions could remain proof against such a persuasive tongue. I overheard this observation and, for a different reason, was moved by it. It was my turn now to lose my heart – and I hoped that the Captain's remark had not been casual blandishment but indicated a deeper interest.

Bill and Peter lived in our drawing room, now untenanted for the duration, and came and went when the spirit, or at least their duties, called them. The huge army boots trod softly among the Persian rugs; manners polished to the shine of the neglected buttons and brass praised Nannie's food, left notes warning of unorthodox comings and goings, made jokes when paths crossed. What their training consisted of, or at least the version of it that the village heard, was strange, mad and exciting. Once their Captain had led them all out of a second storey window. He broke an ankle on impact with the ground, but they followed him none the less, seeming to think this an incident to be ignored. Although gossip said this happened in Moffat, and bolder spirits even pointed out the window in question, I could not help noticing that their Captain, with whom I now had a great deal to do, appeared to be physically intact. But I knew better than to attempt to verify such rumours.

There was, however, substance in the tales of mock encounters, in darkness with live ammunition flashing, on nearby hillsides. Some of our elderly local defenders nearly suffered fatal heart attacks when attempting to patrol the same area of ground. One or two prudently decided to stay at home in the evenings until these brash young men had left us. The instances of German paratroopers having been, unmistakably, encountered up the valley rose spectacularly.

In no time at all Bill and Peter were part of the family. They had been chosen for character, temperament and resourcefulness; they were trained to think for themselves and make their own decisions. They were brave, warm and cheerful, and Bill's solid exterior soon cracked to reveal the gentle kindly man behind it. And one day, when they returned pale and shaken from a session with the Medical Officer, we discovered that they were also human. Standing in line for an injection both our supermen had fainted. I at least could endure my own pinpricks with courage – it was other people's that made me cringe. Quite soon they acquired a communal nickname, based on an appeal in *The Glasgow Herald* for a foster home for two hypothetical waifs, 'Bill and Lizzie'. So they became Bill and Lizzie – and Lizzie never seemed to mind.

They brought their weapons with them and were practising a deadly trade, but they maintained the balance between my mother and Nannie as delicately as if they had been born to it – which they had not. Sometimes Bill spoke of death in the matter of fact tones that indicated deep familiarity with the thought. Peter had a golden haired girl, who came to visit him from Chiswick, and he felt that his physical readiness armoured him against the coming risks.

Not all the time was given up to training. These were also sun-filled summer weeks, the last that I was to be wholly at home. In spare moments Bill and Lizzie sat on the lawn and watched Nannie knit great oiled seaman's stockings or unravel old jerseys to make new ones. I painted their portraits against the pink velvet curtains of our home. And in the evenings there were hops in the Baths Hall.

Such was the spirit of solidarity in the troop that those dances, in contrast to others before and after, were truly egalitarian affairs. From the privates to the Captain everybody went, and each man knew himself the equal of any other. To the considerable apprehension of my mother, who thought of the Baths Hall as the scene of other rank orgies, I went too. I was fathoms deep in love and the whole troop knew I was their Captain's girl. As they regarded me with a kind of protective ownership, so I thought of them as an extension of the brothers I had temporarily lost.

Under the stark light of electric bulbs, on the bare wooden floor, army boots squeaked or thumped to the rhythms of dance bands on the gramophone. For the occasional Scottish reel a piper from the Moffat band played in full Highland dress. There was a familiar smell of overheated khaki wool. Round the walls, on hard wooden chairs, the shyer soldiers sat eyeing possible partners while clusters of girls giggled and ignored them. At the door the air raid wardens had invented excuses concerning blackout regulations for having to oversee what was going on.

It was the first time that I had met many of my Moffat contemporaries on equal terms and I was exhilarated and released. My mother need not have feared for me; though we grasped our opportunities with a febrile gaiety, vividly aware that time was short, the hops were decorous affairs. After the exuberant exertions of reel or polka, waltz or Strip the Willow, couples escaped to the darkness of the High Street, pursued by angry shouts of 'Shut that Door' when a momentary ray of light streamed out. On those evenings the High Street seemed utterly different from its normal peacetime self, infinitely larger since the boundaries of lighted windows were gone, mysteriously moving under the stars with no overlooking eyes to see what was going on.

One weekend the Captain's other girl came up from London to visit him. It was not a shock, he had talked about her. I was curious to see her and to know how I felt. That Saturday night at the hop I discovered objectivity in myself – and in some of the soldiers, notably big dour Bill, a delicate sympathetic tenderness.

'After the ball was over, after the dance was done . . .' was always the final, deeply sentimental tune. I was usually driven home by the Captain. My mother felt the foundations of her world were shaking. She heard the jeep and counted the minutes till the front door shut. However late, she was waiting up – though she tried to pretend it was not for me. We murmured platitudes and said 'goodnight'. Once in my bedroom, joyfully alive, I was still conscious of Nannie in the adjoining room – asleep or awake I did not know. I wondered sometimes whether they worried more about the boys – Robert alone in a remote African district, having to grow a moustache and shave it off again to give himself a fresh face to look at, Laurence and Alastair already facing the hazards of war – or about me drifting, as they saw it, out of their ken because of a man they hardly knew.

Then one day the Commandos left as suddenly as they had come, no-one was supposed to know where. But, inspite of the posters warning us that 'Careless talk costs lives', it had never been impossible to discover destinations, true or suspected. Presently it was asserted that they had gone to tougher hills than the Beef Tub and more arduous circumstances, and there was a feeling of satisfaction that Moffat, at least, had given them a softer summer to remember.

I was at Glencorse Barracks outside Edinburgh, with the Church of Scotland Huts, when in the early spring of 1942 the wireless announced that the submarine base at St Nazaire had been the target of a Commando raid. Casualties were heavy. It was clear, and presently confirmed, that Bill and Lizzie and their companions had been there.

For a short time we hoped they might be prisoners. It seemed impossible that so much preparation and endeavour, so much love and laughter and kindliness, should be removed in the twinkling of an eye. Then we heard that most of them had never even got ashore. Though the Captain and one or two others survived to endure years as POWs, Bill and Lizzie, gunned into the water from their assault boat, died in an inferno of burning oil.

★   ★   ★

The centre of wartime activities in Moffat was the canteen, situated in Well Street in an empty draper's shop. At the beginning there had been two such establishments, but that was before the harsh realities of war brought an end to the village's internal feuds. Now there was only one, and all the women for whom the vital operational activity was to keep homes intact and strong served in it. My mother and Nannie were of this number.

There were two storeys of busy, smoke-filled space, smelling of damp khaki cloth, Woodbines and frying food. Though the regulars, stationed in the town, had their habits, it was never certain when a rush of uniformed strangers, on their way from unknown departure point to uncertain destination, would open the door and pile in demanding instant baked beans and chips. The draper's window now showed the names of all the allied countries and it was surprising how often the quiet sad man sitting in the corner turned out to be from one of them. The world came to Well Street, Moffat, in the war in a way it never had before; and Well Street, Moffat, became familiar with the names of towns and villages in countries covering half the globe whose mention would once have brought bewilderment to most inhabitants' faces.

Not all the men who sat in corners, however, were foreigners brooding on their exile. Once there was an Irishman, with that country's legendary charm, who over a period of some weeks patronised the old shop counter to order a meal and then managed to persuade one of the female helpers, a different one each time, to carry it up the stairs to a quiet side room that he had found. Such favouritism was frowned on, and anyway there was no time to cosset individuals in this way, but always he had a reason that seemed to justify the exception.

It was not until one of the girls, less inhibited than her older sisters, tripped into his lair to find the soldier exposing himself to her that his spare-time hobby was discovered. Then whispered in corners, revealed by blushes, occasionally related with shame, the count of his victims slowly emerged. Too embarrassed by what they had encountered, conscious that their own weakness for flattery had lead them into it, these women had said nothing, always hoping that the next one who disappeared aloft with a plate of beans would actually come down screaming.

Nannie was not one of them. She was not immune to charm, but as a lever it failed to move her. In her brisk, no-nonsense way she had no favourites, and any man who looked for preferential treatment was quickly put in his place. In the shifting alliances and power struggles among the staff she played no part. She was efficient and hard working and in demand for those qualities. Never a member of the WVS, any more than she had been of the Woman's Guild, she nevertheless got special permission to wear their overalls. Once a suggestion was made that she join the canteen committee, but my mother vetoed it. 'Nannie and I can't get out together', was how she voiced her objection. It was not a valid excuse, and Nannie did not consider it such. She suspected that my mother did not like to have a rival. In any case she was content to remain in the background, well knowing how powerful her influence was there. She had some reason for her suspicion, but I think too that my mother lived constantly in anticipation of bad news about her sons, and trusted only Nannie to receive it if she were not herself present when it arrived.

Working in the background was no less arduous than being conspicuously visible. The women who used to help in the house had gone away to war. Nannie, aged forty-six, had been called up but was exempted because my mother was over sixty. Though the contraction which brought her and my mother physically closer together might, in theory, have resulted in fewer chores, in practice the difficulties which shortages imposed, combined with Nannie's natural perfectionism, multiplied rather than reduced the burdens. On Sunday afternoons there was a standing invitation to whichever unit was in the village for six of its soldiers to come to The Lodge, to relax and enjoy Nannie's tea and rock cakes.

Rationing was a challenge to her ingenuity; bargaining across the grocer's counter for scarce goods, while she watched with indignation more favoured customers being given the freedom of the back shop, strained the temper. Making dried eggs into a palatable meal; striving to scrimp and save so that there was some reserve; watching the fuel, cutting down the light, mending, repairing, painting, patching the fabric of the house where now there were no men left to do it, knitting endless boxes of balaclava helmets and other comforts, constantly prepared to stand in when help was needed, working long shifts in the canteen, all this began to undermine her health. Once she nearly fainted, to be rescued by a gallant Polish doctor.

When in the long dark evenings they sat on either side of the fire, for the most part in silence and preoccupied with their thoughts, it was a common past that Nannie and my mother brooded on. Fears for my brothers lurked behind my mother's every thought; a son in Africa, facing heavy responsibilities for which there had hardly been time to prepare him, a son in India with the Japanese knocking at the door, a son in training for work that would put him every night at risk in the air; each morning the news bulletins reported one, two or three of our aircraft unaccounted for – maybe already lost. These were Nannie's children too – and when their individual dreads became too much for them they talked.

It was the fire that was the real cause of friction. For each of them it represented something so personal and profound that of all the things they now had to undertake together tending the fire was perhaps the hardest to share.

My mother sat for long hours gazing into the flames, burning the skin of her legs mottled purple with their heat, confiding in them, taking comfort from the living warmth. When she poked the coals she did so with art and skill. She arranged fresh lumps delicately to make the most of embers dying back. In the mornings she liked to lay the fire herself, convinced that only she knew the secret of a really good blaze. She had the knack, though we sometimes disputed that she was the only one, of drawing a slow grey hearth up into life by holding an opened newspaper across the grate. When at last it caught fire and flared she would crush the flaming sheets imperiously between her hands.

But Nannie too was a superb firemaker. She wove the newspaper crackers that my mother used; she too could coax life out of a dead pile of clinker. She had various personal remedies for an ailing fire and used to infuriate my mother by throwing on potato peelings or kitchen waste. For Nannie, who had been given a poker by her father when she first went into the world, the fire represented her own hearthstone, the independent life that she retained – even though she lived in my mother's house. She too enjoyed poking, arranging, and gazing into the flames. The trouble was that where there had once been two now there was only one hearth.

Each watched the other with a wary eye as the fire between them sighed and crumbled, waiting for moves to pick up the poker. It was not unknown for one to rearrange the efforts of the other. Words were seldom spoken; pursed lips, tuttings, clickings of needles or rustlings of paper and an indrawn breath or two said it all. Of the minor frustrations of the war the sharing of the fire was the one that most sorely tried their nerves.

In the year after St Nazaire I was with the Church of Scotland Huts in Orkney, on the island of Flotta serving the sailors off the battleships anchored in Scapa Flow, and the gunners who protected the land installations. It was a strange, isolated, windswept world, physically very beautiful, where long weeks were spent sustaining the spirits of men waiting for action that never seemed to come; and then, with the silent disappearance of the ships, preparing to comfort and support those who would eventually return from the hell of the Russian convoys round the North Cape. Once, on a day of bitter wind and rain, they came back from a battle, dressed overall for victory. Then we learned that the *Scharnhorst* was sunk.

On Flotta I discovered that the Church's young men could

be just as overbearing when it came to dealing with what they considered subordinate women as junior medical officers. This experience was to lead, after acrimonious discussions with those who worked in offices in Edinburgh, to my taking what were designated 'my rather peculiar talents' to the opposition at the Young Men's Christian Association. There, contrary to the discrimination implicit in their name, the YMCA was prepared to trust their women workers with ultimate authority.

When I came home on leave the euphoria of the early days in Moffat had long passed. Nannie and my mother made special efforts on my behalf; small windfalls, carefully hoarded, were produced. Some separation again took place, for each liked to talk to me on her own, freer to question or confide if the other was not at hand to hear.

My mother felt that the war was taking us from her, in a sense more far-reaching than necessary physical absence. Though she never wholly recognised it, nothing took us from her. We remained inextricably part of her blood and spirit, carrying with us everywhere we went the unmistakable stamp of her conscience and her concern. Nannie, less intimately involved, had not expected us to stay – and every return which included her was to be treasured without misgiving.

But it was true that, while my mother looked back to a past about whose re-creation in the future she had as many fears as hopes, I had found in the war a freedom long sought, and there were aspects of that life I did not wish to reveal, nor was I willing to make too plain my enjoyment of much of it. Perhaps it was when Alastair came on leave, operational now, accepting of their care, ready to be gentle and to laugh with them, enjoying the quietness of the house which he loved, concealing as they did the pain and fear that lay just outside the magic circle of its garden, that the two women who loved him felt closest to each other and most at ease.

It was in 1944, not long after D-day and his twenty-first birthday, when we had begun to breathe again, that one morning his aeroplane did not come home. I was running a sailor's hostel up the Gareloch when my mother telephoned to ask me to meet her in Glasgow. She was calm and controlled and I did not guess until I saw her what had happened.

The telegram said missing. Miss Rennie who had written it out in her clear script and sent it up to The Lodge had had the news before my mother did. The whole village treated her with kindly hopefulness. My mother's anguish was Nannie's concern, through which she could ease her own sorrow; for my mother I would have afforded a similar outlet, but I could not come home.

For weeks she and Nannie consoled each other with surface optimism, concealing pessimism and pain beneath recollection – and speculation about his present circumstances. A very tall young man with large feet, he had had to have all his shoes made for him since he was sixteen. The suffering that he might be caused in a prisoner of war camp by being improperly shod preoccupied my mother; Nannie wondered who would feed him adequately if he was trying to make his escape through occupied Europe. They spoke of things he liked to eat, of his cheerful temperament, of daredevil rides on his motorbike, anything that showed his ability to survive. In the long evenings by the fire, when like a bubble slowly surfacing from the depths of a pool a remark broke the silence, the talk concerned the living boy in need of consolation. He had not yet taken his place in the past.

Then one day all doubts were dispelled. He had been the pilot, and eventually a member of his crew did come home through Spain. They had jumped from a crippled plane by parachute, my brother last. By that time it was too low and too late.

In the desperation of her grief my mother left the home where memories were still an agony rather than a solace and went to stay with a sister. Alone in the big house, as in crises she had so often been, Nannie handled enquiries, answered the telephone, and worked to ease her own pain. She understood and admired my mother too well to feel deserted. It was my mother who wrote almost immediately to apologise for not sufficiently recognising that Nannie's too was a family grief. It was one which Nannie preferred to come to terms with on her own.

*   *   *

When the war ended I was with the YMCA in charge of a canteen in Lille, in northern France. It was not a moment of exhilaration, but rather of sadness, exhaustion and regret. So much seemed to have been lost, and as yet I could not see the gains clearly. It was to be another year before I came home; a year spent running the large YMCA canteen in Nijmegen close to the German border with Holland.

Nijmegen was on the main route from the Channel ports to Hamburg. The town had been badly bombed and for the civilian population everything was in short supply. It was a Canadian area, so many of our regulars came from that country. They were open-hearted and immensely generous. On the main road outside the canteen, by courtesy of the Canadians, a huge sign indicated our presence. In the two bottom corners a St Andrew's Cross and a Welsh Dragon blazoned forth the nationalities of myself and my colleague. To thousands of soldiers travelling to and from Germany we became a well-known and welcome stopping place.

It was a time of slow demobilisation, of the disillusion of a war finished and a peace not yet begun; of great anxiety in case the longed for return home should after all prove illusory. As the Canadians went and a homesick British remnant remained, we redoubled our efforts to feed, comfort, counsel and entertain them. A Signals Unit wished to run a magazine and enlisted our help. I said they could have it on condition that I was appointed their Agony Aunt. The result was a success for them; and for me the fulfilment of a secret ambition. In a dreary February we created Valentine cards for wives and sweethearts, discovering a talent for nostalgic verse. On my birthday, in April, a dozen or so of those who used our facilities regularly bought a whole barrowload of Dutch flowers – the one commodity still to be had in abundance – and gave it to me as a present.

Sometimes, if he was passing near Moffat, I would give a soldier my mother's address and suggest he call with news of her daughter – or perhaps, by some of Nannie's cosseting, to break the shock I suspected he was about to get on returning home. At intervals I came myself.

For me the contrast was very great. In Moffat too a mood of uncertainty prevailed. It was true the war had ended – but much had been lost, for my mother and Nannie a whole world that could never be the same again. The officers and men of the 48th Division Battle School, stationed in the town, had invited Nannie to a party of thanks and celebration. She did not go. The background had become her natural province and she had little inclination to leave it, though she was proud to have been invited. She put away the souvenirs of her wartime service as carefully as she had the mementoes of the happy times before all her babies grew up.

The house was quiet and shabby, heavy with memories of the past. I talked of my activities, but the setting in which they took place seemed a long way away and my enjoyment of them only added to fears that I too would not come back. Once, to my shame, I returned to Holland two days early, sitting consumed with guilt on the floor of a battered draughty Dakota, trying to suppress the shiver of pleasure I felt at being in the thick of things again.

The next few years were filled with perplexities. I came back at last to echoes of childhood and attempts to reassemble the peaceful picture of our youth in a jigsaw puzzle whose pieces had been ruthlessly scattered when we had gone away. Coming home no longer meant the same thing as once it had. When Laurence was demobbed from India, his one desire was to make a new life for himself in a country of kinder skies and less exhausted gloom. We were restless and unhappy, wanting only to leave again, to start to build new and separate existences for ourselves. My mother saw and dreaded this though she would do nothing to stop us.

Nannie herself began once more to think of passing her responsibilities back to me. Fifty-one was not too old to seek fresh nurseries and begin again. Perhaps this difficult decision would actually have been made but for one thing. After eight years Robert came home from Africa, married and with a child.

It was a cold winter when again there was a baby in the house. Once more there were two firesides. Nannie had returned to her own room. For my sister-in-law, meeting for the first time a mother-in-law known only through correspondence, the addition of a Nannie so deeply embedded in our family history must have presented a formidable ordeal. For her part Nannie, her professional instincts still acute inspite of long years in abeyance, was quick to appreciate that attitudes must differ where a grandchild was concerned. She got out the hoarded relics of the days when we had all been infants which, squirrel-like, she had salted away. Nannie, who so lightly parted with many of the things we treasured, had herself wrapped and carefully laid aside in safe and secret places particularly cherished milestones of our journey through childhood. Now with surprise, I saw again a beautifully clad doll that I had long forgotten, small dresses folded in tissue paper, special toys that we had once loved, produced for the delectation of my niece and the approval of her mother.

Nannie was an anachronism now. The new generation of young mothers was ready to accept many compromise solutions to lighten the burden of caring for their children, but Nannies who had been given – and gladly undertook as ours had done – an equal responsibility in this task were out of fashion. So she busied herself with her household jobs, which had not become less onerous, and stayed quietly in her room waiting for offers of help to be taken up – well aware of the priorities to be accorded to parents and grandmother. She did not have long to wait. It was soon clear that she had not lost her gift; that where others sometimes failed she could still comfort, relieve, train and entertain a small child.

But she had to walk delicately, not with my sister-in-law, only too glad to find willing help at hand, but with my mother, free to make the most of her grandchild in a way that had not been possible when my father was alive and she had borne her own. As she had not been when we were young, my mother was jealous now of her pre-eminence.

For a while the post-war life seemed to return to a natural progression, ignoring the dislocation that had taken place. Once more there was coming and going in the house, and times when it echoed again to fun and laughter and voices making plans. Laurence went to South Africa, from where eventually he too came back to visit with a wife. The grandchildren when they arrived were passing swallows, never present long enough to bring back summer – nevertheless to Nannie holding out a hope.

I had returned to study, coming home from London as I had done from school for holidays; taking my mother away sometimes with me, conspiring with Nannie to bring her happiness – reminded always by my mother that Nannie should not be neglected. All the same I was the reason for displacing her again.

I wanted a studio. If I must be at home, I needed space to paint. The night nursery, which adjoined my bedroom and for all those years had been a source of irritation to me, seemed admirably adapted to this purpose. So Nannie was uprooted and flung like a castaway into the spare room that had sheltered the Polish Count and many other guests besides. She went, uncomplaining, and it never occurred to me that I was robbing her of twenty-six years occupation and all the physical memories that a particular setting had accumulated.

Once I brought home an African friend, the first man of his continent that Nannie had met – indeed Moffat too had not seen many of his race. A crowd of little boys followed us to church, speculating loudly on the question of his colour. Nannie was more discreet. She came to me quietly and asked anxiously if it would come off on her pristine white sheets. My mother had more apprehensive questionings which at the time I never guessed. Nor did she reveal them to me, though it is possible she did to Nannie. She thought I had made up my mind to marry him.

In this she was wrong, but perhaps something in my manner misled her for I wanted very much to marry the young man who had introduced us to each other.

When my brothers had come home the possibility of moving our mother out of the big house had become an object of silent pressure and the subject of open discussion.

We all wanted it, I suspect, a good deal more than she did. Nannie we did not consult. There were good and valid reasons, as strong it seemed for my mother's welfare as for our convenience. Demonstrably, and on this we all agreed, our house was too big. Moffat was becoming more isolated, already the small branch line on which we used to take our miniature journeys with Nannie was closed. Our own visits were now intermittent and our priorities diluted by other preoccupations. In the long winter months it pained us to think of Nannie and my mother sitting alone, remote and waiting, thinking of us; how much better for everyone if they were in Edinburgh, easily reachable, able to start afresh within the orbit of a wide range of new activities and interests. It seemed a good analysis at the time.

My wedding was to be the last great party of our Moffat life.

Before that happened, however, I took a trip to West Africa to see if I could accommodate myself to the lifestyle of my intended bridegroom who worked there. That was the real reason, though I said I was going to paint, to visit my brothers, to enlarge my experience – putting forward a smokescreen to deflect too close a scrutiny from a resolve not yet for public view.

I do not think I deceived my mother, nor indeed Nannie. In the weeks before I departed, by banana boat from Liverpool, our home was filled with unspoken questions, oblique references which told me of my mother's unhappiness, the long silences when on either side it seemed impossible to approach the truth. We were indeed too close for comfort. Then I would go to Nannie, to talk of trivialities, knowing that she accepted that I had to go and would not burden me with any obligations; that she never judged and rarely criticised. The debts indeed were on my side, though I barely recognised them. It was her presence that made my departure possible. The last evening I sat between them at a concert and listened to the heavenly singing of the Vienna Boys' Choir. Of the three of us I think it was only Nannie who enjoyed it.

I returned engaged. My mother met me with smiles and loving congratulations; to Nannie she said, 'I've lost her'. It was not true. It was never to be true; nevertheless she felt it to be so at the time and Nannie was the only person to whom she could make this feeling known. Nannie understood what lay behind it; Nannie knew and admired the strength of will with which she would conceal her despair from me and Nannie would not, as relatives might, either mock or chide her.

Mine was to be a Moffat wedding, a celebration of all those years of youth and childhood, now finally to be left behind. Nannie F's family lent us their large and beautiful house and its mistress, my mother's oldest friend created my bouquet. The roly-poly baker in Well Street made the wedding cake, the hotel in the High Street did the catering. Everything that could be done in Moffat was done. Because I had no brothers at home my mother was to give me away. Nannie made my wedding dress.

Clothes rationing had only just ceased. Fine material was hard to obtain. When I took her the yards of pale blue-green crepe-de-chine she was nervous. It was a long time since she had last dressed me for a big occasion and wartime restrictions had diverted her energies from delicate stitching. She looked at the folds of soft material billowing across her table and hesitated. Her fingers were roughened from the years of kitchen toil; for the first time I noticed that her abundant hair was turning grey. But she had never refused a challenge, and she did not now. In the afternoons and evenings, when the work of keeping the household turning over was finished, she sat at her table cutting and basting, the hand machine whirring as a dart was finely stitched, gathers eased into place, tiny rolled hems handsewn, invisible to all except the two who knew them to be there.

Looking towards the golf course, Moffat

Each time I went for a fitting her eye was keen and critical. She liked to be praised, but only when the praise was just – and no-one was a better judge of that than she was. Nothing passed that was not perfect. Though others might admire when I walked up the aisle, she was the one for whom knowledge would make the difference between mediocrity or perfection. When it was done I could have worn it inside out, so meticulous was the finishing of her work, even in all the secret places where it would never be seen.

Nannie helped me to dress and it was to her, as so often in our family, certain of a loving ear and sealed lips, that I confided my final trepidations. When I galloped down the aisle after the ceremony, shocking the congregation by the speed with which I signalled my relief that it was safely over, my mother was full of foreboding that I was going for good. Nannie never doubted that I would be back.

WINTER

The move to Edinburgh was made some months before my marriage. In my relief that this transaction had been safely accomplished, I overlooked the pain which parting with the home of twenty-nine years must bring to these two women whom I loved. It had been the background to my mother's marriage and to more than half Nannie's lifetime; the centre of so much happiness and shared experience. For both of them Moffat was to remain the focus of their most treasured memories.

Nannie, however, was plunged into the minutiae of moving, listing, sorting, arranging, packing in a way that only she could. While my mother, with great efficiency, made room plans and labelled furniture, took decisions about carpets, books, pictures, ornaments, it was Nannie who knew to the last detail the particulars of linen, china, glass, silver, cutlery, kitchenware, cushion covers and curtains, in which boxes they were packed and where, once safely in the new house, they would go.

In Edinburgh I scrubbed and scoured, and supervised the decorating. Colour and its personal affinities had always struck me as mysterious. Why was it that human personality responded in differing ways to varying colours? In my own room, as soon as I was old enough to have a choice, I had surrounded myself with the yellows, browns and greens that were the opposite of my mother's pinks and blues. I can never have consulted Nannie about the decoration of her new sitting room. I gave her the background in which I myself felt happiest and made it green. As soon as she could she redecorated it to suit her own wishes, which accorded more nearly with my mother's.

Though she should have seen it as the compliment it was, my mother was often irritated by the visible influence she exerted on Nannie's taste. Gradually over the years, but with an impeccable sense of what would harmonise with her own physique and personality, Nannie's clothes, in colour and cut, began to resemble my mother's. In looks and figure they were very different people, the one tall and commanding, the other petite; it was Nannie's own natural discrimination that made the transference successful. When dressed to go out, in the blues and greys that my mother so much liked, she achieved a style which, while it owed a clear debt, was none the less distinctively her own. But watching her disappear down the road my mother would sometimes tut with annoyance, and I knew from the look on her face that she felt herself in some way – unnecessarily – diminished.

Though much smaller, the Edinburgh house still provided room for Nannie and my mother to have their separate hearths. The fires that burned there were sacrosanct; each liked to clean and set her own. The kitchen was Nannie's domain; my mother ruled in the small connecting pantry. Each washed her own dishes.

Sometimes, returning for a visit, I would speculate on the division that lay between them, and regret that human beings were so difficult to fit in to the ordered patterns that seem to the outsider to offer aid, comfort and compactness. But then I was not an outsider, and even while I thought this I knew that change was not possible. These arrangements, product of a lifetime together, gave them the strength of solitariness, buttressed by the knowledge that they were not alone, surrounded by the cement of a common past vividly present, whether in silence or in speech.

To some extent the garden replaced the rivalry of the fire. In Moffat the sprawl of lawns and trees, flower beds and vegetable plot, was Wattie's kingdom. My mother rarely trespassed on it; Nannie not at all. But in the small compact squares of earth which surrounded the Edinburgh house my mother began to find a source of peace and refreshment. So too did Nannie. The elderly man who came once a week to cut the grass and deal with heavier jobs was no more talented than Wattie when it came to flowers. But now, working on an intimate scale, my mother, encouraged by initial small successes, started to cultivate the ground. And Nannie, whose father had loved gardening, found at hand outside her kitchen door patches of earth waiting only for tender care to grow rich with blooms.

They never worked together, nor did they consult each other about horticultural plans. But under their shared endeavours the garden flourished. Nannie bought packets of seeds. Wherever she scattered them, they grew. She transplanted bowls of withered winter bulbs from the house to any outdoor space that offered them room. The next year they multiplied gloriously. If she brought back from a holiday a shrivelled root, it took heart from her tending and in no time at all was putting out fresh shoots. As she had cared for children, so Nannie cared for her plants – and like the children they responded.

The house was square and plain, built of grey stone. Nannie was its major domo. Though not extensive, the work of the household was more than she could manage alone. Two mornings each a week Mrs W and Mrs A came in to help. Mrs W was plump and self-contained with a tragic personal history revealed only allusively over a cup of tea or when helping to shake out blankets in the sun. She was conscientious and hard working, amenable to Nannie's perfectionist fervour. Mrs A was scatty, unpunctual and voluble. Like an astute slave master Nannie drove her to tasks in which she would have encouraged Mrs W.

Both knew that it was not possible to take advantage of her all-seeing eye or her supreme regard for my mother's interest; nor could they accuse her of sitting idly by while they worked. It was Nannie who washed the windows and turned out the cupboards, who dealt with recalcitrant tradesmen and supported my mother when she reluctantly engaged in verbal battles. It was Nannie who spring cleaned, patched and painted, mended fuses and allowed no shelf to conceal a store of unpolished silver, unmended linen or forgotten dirty glass. It was her pride to be able to lay her hands on anything that was asked of her, to know that any casual visitor would find my mother's house in immaculate order. It was also, and increasingly, a burden on her health.

But, however much it filled her days, the care of the house was not enough. As she had not changed her name, so her nature remained the same. To us she was Nannie, and within her the dream of new nurseries remained alive still. When Laurence's family began to arrive he suggested that she might come to South Africa to look after them.

She was in her later fifties. It was forty years since she had first left home to go to work in London; for thirty-five years she had been with my mother. She wanted to go, there would have been a deep satisfaction in looking after the fledglings of one of her 'birds'. Had they been nearer home perhaps she could have made the transfer.

She began to try to sever the strands of the web that bound

her not only to my mother but to our home; to detach herself from the familiar landscape of remembrance. I am not sure that she did not, once again, take out her suitcases and place them conspicuously where both she and we could take them as the sign of a decision slowly maturing into action. She thought of the joys of looking after babies; then remembered the fresh obligations that had been laid upon her by my marriage. She saw clearly that there might be gains for both in a separation from my mother; but the old loyalty to my father had not yet lost its power to keep her to an unspoken promise. She admired my mother, but was contemptuous of her ability to manage the practical aspects of her life alone.

If my mother could have brought herself to say a word the web might have been broken and she might indeed have gone. But my mother did not find it possible to say that word. She was torn between the chafing of too tight bonds and the knowledge of all that had served to draw them so close. She too placed a high regard on loyalty, though if Nannie had gone to my brother there need have been no sundering of ties. She depended on Nannie's management of her household affairs, nevertheless she was a woman of strong character who was quite capable of overcoming any difficulties as they occurred. But she shrank from the loss of the other half of what had become their joint life. Like trees of different species, growing by chance too near each other, the branches of their experience had become so inextricably intertwined that the prospect of separation seemed to carry the risk of mutilation.

So the suitcases were put away, and the grandchildren came home to visit and to grow accustomed, as we had done, to take Nannie for granted as part of the family.

When they were still quite young Robert's children returned to Scotland to school. Their grandmother's house became their second home. As casually as though they were stepping on to a bus, they grew accustomed to shuttling over continents with a label round their necks. Once more Nannie packed and repacked school trunks, washed, ironed and mended, annoyed my niece – as she had annoyed me – by tidying away school clothes the instant she got her hands on them making no allowances for any personal decisions as to whether they were needed in the holidays or not.

Times change, and so with time do people. Elements of situations once known are shaken up and redistributed. Basic features may remain the same, the designs that they reform into do not. These children were not Nannie's children, as we had been. The authority that we had accorded her had no reality for them. My mother, though granting Nannie's expertise, professed now to have some expertise of her own. In the more relaxed atmosphere of altered circumstances and differing mores the framework in which we had been brought up no longer appertained. Only when tempers frayed and childish passions exploded did my mother acknowledge that Nannie's was the firmer guiding hand, that it was she who still possessed the ability to calm small agitated minds, to counter obstinacy and distract obsession.

When she had entered her seventies my mother, who had never travelled much, decided to pay a visit to the African continent to see her sons and their families. Though later she was to fly, on this first occasion she went by ship. Such was her ignorance of the delights and dangers of a long sea voyage that when the vessel struck a bad storm, smashing furniture and crockery and injuring a number of passengers, my mother alone appeared at breakfast in the restaurant making plain to the astonished steward that she thought this was normal weather on the great oceans.

She left Nannie, with a cheque book of signed blank cheques, in charge of the Edinburgh house. At that moment the friction of too close contact melted away and the foundation of their relationship – trust – was revealed to both of them.

Nannie too, in those years, stepped outside her normal life to make a journey. After much urging she went to Canada for seven weeks, to visit her elder sister and her family. As habit often conceals us from our inmost selves, so dramatic change can result in personal revelations. Perhaps it was this journey which, in a sense, brought Nannie back to her own people; that uncovered in her the strength to make alterations if she so wished.

We saw her off, my mother and myself, at the railway station in Edinburgh. She was dressed with taste and style, her white hair laid in wings beneath her hat, her stubbly chin brushing mine as she hugged me and said goodbye. Beside her were two neat suitcases, no doubt packed with the same care and attention as were those of the grandchildren who had left for Africa the day before. We wished her well and turned for home, my mother and I, our load of guilt lightened for a while.

I think we wondered whether Nannie would come back. Postcards told us that she was enjoying herself immensely. It was a new world; she was welcomed and fêted. 'They all have cars', she wrote, 'even the cleaning woman'. Mrs A and Mrs W would have been surprised. She was interested in everything. New plants and flowers intrigued her. She examined new domestic arts and crafts with a skilled eye, admiring the technology of Canadian kitchens, got to know her young relatives. She even began to reassess her own character, boldly taking a ride on Lake Huron in her nephew's boat – which his own mother had never done – and telling me that she had decided that she was not after all as timid as my father had liked to pretend.

She came back full of this experience – but not sorry to be again in Scotland. Strengthened by a fresh perspective and the support of her relatives, she had begun to think of a small home of her own. She was in her late sixties and long past retirement age. Six years before my brothers and I had given her a television set to mark forty years with us. For some time she had known that all was not well with her health. She would wake up in the early morning hours with her heart fluttering and creep downstairs to make herself a cup of tea and crouch over the electric fire. High blood pressure and uneasy sensations in her chest had frightened her, her eyes were dimming. Gradually she had begun to want to be her own woman.

It was not to be an easy or a speedy break. My mother, though active and dominant, was in her eighties. Her sisters found it difficult to conceive that Nannie might leave her. The old loyalties had not weakened, but weariness, a sense of slowing down, the pull of a little place of her own, all began to tip the scales. Though torn by feelings of betrayal, Nannie knew that I supported her. It was time to part. My mother, in her heart, must have known it too, but long habit made it hard for her to acknowledge this truth.

In the years in the Edinburgh house, on my visits home, my mother would meet me at the front door, having sat with one eye on the clock and one in the window for some time before I was actually due. Within the house, in her own sitting room, Nannie waited for me to come and greet her. As time had gone on, and the grandchildren ceased to be central to their lives, much of the focus of day to day affairs became for each the other. So I would find myself listening to the narration of domestic incidents, often the same one from two different angles, with a reenactment of liberties taken, lapses of memory denied, misunderstandings, accidents (which one side or the other had hoped would be concealed from me), the reactions of visitors, small triumphs achieved at the other's expense.

But always, in the end, each would urge on me my love and loyalty and duty to the other. My mother would say 'Have you been to see Nannie?', and I would hardly dare to admit that I already had, lest she be affronted that I had thought of it myself, that my own affection had taken me into that other sitting room rather than her care for Nannie's inalienable rights. Nannie would exhort me to look after my mother, to remember that she was growing old – though it was still to be many years before my mother herself would admit this fact and such an admonition, had she known of it, would have greatly angered her.

I spent long hours striving to interpret and transmit their points of view, to prise them asunder without inflicting pain, wrestling myself with love and guilt and fear of hurting. They found it difficult to live together, though neither could yet understand how they could live apart. To the end my mother found reasons, which seemed to her good, why Nannie should stay. She went all the same, to a cottage near a niece in the country from which she had first come, and to a winter flowering.

When Nannie left she did not cease to feel herself deeply involved in our family affairs, which were truly her family affairs also. She scanned the papers, including the *Moffat News* which my mother sent on to her, with an eagle eye for clippings that might be of interest to us. She had an astonishing capacity for discovering, recording and passing on items we would never otherwise have seen, both family and local. For her part my mother was constantly on the telephone asking where her best pillow slips were, or the large pudding plates, or how to deal with the boiler in the kitchen. She never failed to get an exact and helpful answer. Not only household queries went back and forth; family news, our comings and goings, were faithfully passed on.

When I came up from London to visit, Nannie was summoned to tea and sat, almost for the first time, in the sitting room between us recalling old days. Her memory was matchless; in argument she never contradicted – but she was rarely converted and her face showed clearly when she disagreed. Invariably she produced from her handbag a scrap of printed paper containing some fascinating titbit that we had failed to notice, while my mother eyed her clothes with a faint return of the old irritation.

In 1971 my mother celebrated her 90th birthday. Robert arranged a lunch party for all her family and friends. At first my mother was hesitant; she did not want to be singled out, she feared the strain would be too much, she had nothing to wear. Later I discovered that the ceremonial marking of this anniversary held for her an unpleasant significance. Until this moment she had taken no pride in her age, indeed she had ignored it. Active and independent, it did not seem to matter what year the birthdays ticked off. But suddenly, when her whole world began to draw attention to this milestone in her life and to impress on her the wonder of reaching her ninth decade, she was compelled for the first time to recognise that she was old.

We assured her that the occasion would be no strain. We would see that the hotel had a regal chair available, in which she could sit while we brought up to her those to whom she wished to speak. She received this suggestion with a snort; then, a few days later, announced to us that she was, on the contrary, going to make a speech.

It was a December day, clear and bright. We were all there, her sons and daughter with their spouses, her grandchildren, sisters and brother, nieces and nephews, cousins, great-nieces and nephews, old friends; from Moffat, Wattie and Jean and others to whom she had become a matriarch and a legend. And there was Nannie.

Perhaps of all those present Nannie, more than any, knew the inwardness of the events that had shaped my mother's life. In times of stress she had often preferred Nannie's detachment to the more emotional support of her family. In the long years together, knowing that she could trust her, my mother had revealed much to Nannie. She had come through many sorrows as well as much happiness, and Nannie had come through them with her. Her admiration for my mother was steadfast and unstinting – though it was not blind.

As usual, dressed impeccably, Nannie took her place among us at the 90th birthday. She knew us all, family, relations and old friends, and was accepted by everyone as an HR by adoption. She eyed my mother in her nannyish way and said to me 'She'll be getting tired – you ought to make her sit down', knowing quite well that I would never try – and probably knowing also how it would have annoyed my mother if she had seen us fussing over her.

'I've always cared for people and I don't intend to stop now', Nannie had told me once. I did not attempt to stop her, my role as usual was to hold the balance even. I had become better at it with the years. Age and a life of my own had resolved many frustrations and my understanding of and admiration for them both had grown.

My mother made her speech. For fifteen minutes, without a note, she stood up and spoke with warmth, gratitude and humour, and a memory that had not yet failed. She was congratulated and toasts were drunk. Bathing quietly in the reflected glory Nannie too came in for her share of compliments. My husband teased her and she bridled with pleasure. She kept a sharp eye on the hotel staff and the practical arrangements of the reception. It was her instinct to care, to manage, to put right, and there was no occasion on which such habitual reflexes were laid to rest.

When the time came for the gathering to disperse and we all went back to our separate houses, Nannie took the train for the little cottage that was now her home.

She climbed the steep hill from Polmont railway station and turned right at the top. Her house was one of a row looking on to an unmade road. It was very small; in apple pie order. Before she moved in everything had been modernised, a bathroom installed where there had been none before and cooking facilities updated. For the first time in her life she had things exactly as she wanted them. In the grate her own fire blazed bright, on the mantelpiece the familiar pictures of us as children were ranged. Looking round I saw many objects that I knew. The chair in which, at four months old, she had nursed me night and day with a pillow tied to her arm to protect my painful head stood on one side of the fire. The Doulton china figure of a balloon woman that I had lusted after when I was about fourteen – and then abandoned – smiled from the top of a cupboard beside a row of my books. The television set we had given her to celebrate forty years as our Nannie had a little table of its own. There was a yellow china frog, with a vast open mouth to take flowers of which my brother Alistair had been fond; near it his photograph in Flight Lieutenant's uniform. It was not only Nannie's life that was in this little room, it was also mine.

Behind the objects, each with its specific memory of a moment in our common past, lay all the wide arena of two human lifetimes which, for a space of fifty years or more, had come together. I remembered myself as I had been when the balloon woman filled up all my dreams. I knew now that Nannie had quite different images and recollections of that time of which I had no knowledge. The grave little girl with ringlets on her shoulders, caught with her brothers in a studied pose, was Nannie's baby; but I, who out of a multitude of experiences felt myself to have created quite a different persona, was a stranger to this child still living in Nannie's memory. And yet, at the points where we came together in our re-creation of the past, the divergence of our visions, in which there was no conflict, gave richness and perspective to the presence of those everyday objects.

Essential things within me had not changed. I felt at ease with Nannie's knowledge of my inner self. There was no need to bow to the pressures of deep familial love or assume any temporary disguise. Her own unchanging image in my eyes accommodated my altered habits, looks and tastes. And between us we had one bond whose strength in both our lives was undiminished by the passing of time, the memory of my youngest brother. We had known and loved him for the fullness of his life. No later growth had thickened to shelter and conceal the boy we knew. The snapshots of the kilted imp, the ten-year old stretched out beside his dog, the handsome flyer, which lay in Nannie's drawers, linked us to him and through him to each other.

Everything in the little house was spotless, shining and sparkling with a sheen that was peculiarly Nannie's – and which I had never been able to emulate in my own home. I knew that if I opened all the cupboards in her kitchens, or glanced inside the oven, I would find exactly the same immaculate interiors. All this although her sight was beginning to fail, and too strenuous endeavours could leave her sick and shaken.

She always gave me tea, the kettle singing on the iron hob

attached to the top bar of the grate. The sandwiches were daintily cut, her own scones laid out to tempt me, with butter and home-made jam. I teased her gently about the butter knife, long since abandoned by later generations. The china would have met with my mother's approval, she might have chosen it herself. On the sideboard were some of the old nursery plates with their red and blue flowered border. Mistress in her own home, Nannie urged me as she always had done to feed up and look after myself.

Everywhere there were plants, growing sturdily, blooming exotically, being coaxed from undernourished weaklings into robust health. They stood in corners where, had they been mine, lack of light would have caused them to wilt. They clung to northern window sills as though all the warmth of the southern sun were there. Whether common or rare, they grew as though the expertise of Kew was at their disposal.

But it was when we went through the tiny kitchen into the long thin exposed garden that the triumphs of Nannie's green fingers were made manifest. Great cushions of bloom in many different colours filled the beds; small flowering bushes blazed in pink or crimson, drifts of white alyssum were banked like snow. Across the farther end the decorative firs that she had planted as a screen were doing their best to grow at her behest. The trillium bulbs brought from Canada had made themselves at home. A winter flowering jasmine, when the fragile flowerets covered its bare branches, paralleled her own late blossoming. Looking to either side it was clear that not so long before this patch of land had been rough field; now she could have opened it to public scrutiny – and charged what price she pleased.

Though fine sewing was no longer possible Nannie continued to knit. Her skilled hands had lost none of their cunning and barely needed eyesight to guide their path. Packed away in boxes, lying in tissue paper, were small garments, dressed dolls, or blue and yellow stuffed bears, waiting for the appearance of the next great-grandchild,

122

ready for her own great-nieces and nephews, or any other baby whose provenance she knew. Carefully treasured also, produced for my inspection, was the orange net and taffeta dress, with cross lacing on the bodice, in which aged twelve I had gone to my brother's school dance. Now colleagues in the school where Nannie's niece, Margaret, taught a new generation regarded with awe the fairy lightness of the hand stitching.

Paradoxically, all her life Nannie had been alone and independent, and she did not intend to relinquish this status now. Margaret kept an eye on her, but Nannie still fought her own battles. The unmade road, on to which the cottage looked, was a source of constant friction between the authorities and the small community: neighbours, who kept a menagerie in a dwelling barely large enough for two human beings and who had been known to threaten reprisals if action were taken against them, caused her much anxiety – but did not daunt her spirit. But for her sight she would have made a return visit to Canada, instead she had to be content with seeing Canadian relatives who came to Scotland. She remained, as always, passionately interested in all our doings.

My mother began to fail when she was well into her nineties. She went to live with Robert on the Clyde and the Edinburgh house was sold. Nannie asked if she could have the pair of highly polished brass shell cases, from the first World War, which for all the years they had known each other had stood beside my mother's fire holding poker, brush and tongs. Now, symbolically, when my mother no longer had use for them, they guarded Nannie's grate and held the poker that her father had made for her.

Each Christmas, until my mother died aged ninety-eight, our family met at my brother's home to celebrate. Usually there were grandchildren present, once a great-grandchild. Nannie was there too. The age gap which had long been closed, had begun to open again. For the first time I realised that fifteen years separated Nannie from my mother.

Nannie

Nannie brought her knitting, latterly coloured squares to make up into beautiful blankets. She sat beside my mother, as she had at picnics, upright and busy, making few concessions to the mood of relaxation around her, keeping a watchful eye on all of us. At eighty-two she still felt it wrong to be idle and though her semi-blindness made some jobs impossible, unobtrusively and without fuss she helped my sister-in-law whenever she could. Once, looking at her and thinking of her total devotion to our family, I said, 'What a strange life you must have had Nannie'. She stared at me with her large half-blind eyes. It was clear that she did not share my view of her vocation. 'Well there's one thing I've always been grateful for', she said, 'all my life I was trusted'. It seemed indeed a proud epitaph.

They sat beside each other, warily, these two old ladies – and I sat with them keeping the balance still. In my mother's memory only the days far back remained, before Nannie or her children had swum into her ken. It was not a time with which Nannie was unfamiliar, for she had heard those old tales often retold. It was my mother who distrusted her half-heard interventions, who said to me testily when Nannie raised her voice, 'I'm not deaf. Why is she shouting at me?' And Nannie, whose affection for her was deeply rooted in years of mutual trust, would look at me and fall silent.

There is a rivalry inherent in many long close partnerships which does not vanish with old age. Indeed unwelcome weakness may intensify it; the struggle to retain an identity fast slipping away can make painful the sight of others still able to hold their own in the continuing battle. Till very near the end my mother kept the strong sense of her individual life that she had always had, and it was in the nature of their relationship that there should be clashes with Nannie, who had never herself been subservient.

Nevertheless, when she was not there, my mother often asked, 'Where is Nannie?' The last time they saw each other the long loyalty and dependence reasserted itself. It was a cold, dark December evening. Nannie was to leave next day.

124

At 9.30 p.m. she said to my mother, 'I'm going upstairs – would you like to come?'

My mother assented. Her grandson heaved her out of her chair and gave her the stick that supported her. The two old people left the room together, walking side by side, not touching. My mother had forgotten who her grandson was and, as always, sought information from Nannie about the unknown young man.

At the top of the stairs, panting, she stopped. Then they moved on, very slowly, to the door of her room. My mother looked around. 'Where are you Nannie? Where are you?'

'I'm only next door'.

'Oh, that's good. I don't want to disturb you in the night but I may have to'.

Those were the last words between them. The next day Nannie left and by the following Christmas my mother was dead. They had known each other sixty-one years.

'I still feel', Nannie said, 'that I let your father down'. She meant by leaving my mother when she did, but I well knew, and could reassure her, that any bond which she felt outstanding had been amply redeemed.

I gave Nannie some of my mother's scarves and gloves, and a grey fur shoulder cape. The next Christmas she sat in my mother's chair. She took it as of right; we gave it as her due. I could not help wondering how my mother would have viewed such a usurpation.

Nannie had returned to her own family now. The little cottage was sold and she had moved into a flat a few doors from her niece Margaret. Known as Aunt Jo, and renowned for her lively memory, our Nannie was now consulted by young Marshall descendents about their own family history.

But ever since we had left Moffat Nannie had gone back there regularly for her holiday and it was our family history that had at last become truly her own. When the trains no longer stopped at Beattock, on the main line, she went by bus. Long after we had left it was Nannie who kept alive the family presence in the village, who relayed news between those who still remembered the HRs and ourselves, who took again her place as Nannie HR.

She did not go alone. She had in any case, friends in Moffat and many for whom she was still a known and respected figure. One day, in Edinburgh, in a household accident, she had broken her ankle. The ambulance which took her to the hospital picked up en route another elderly victim. They lay side by side and became firm friends. For many years afterwards, into very old age, Nannie and Miss Syme descended annually on Moffat.

The return to Moffat was a refreshment, a plunge back into scenes among which Nannie had been very happy. She did not mind the changes. There were, of course, physical transformations, but small country towns alter their basic structures slowly. The two old ladies stayed in the High Street, in the old coaching inn which had become the Balmoral Hotel, now sparkling white with new anachronistic shutters.

During the last few years many American visitors had discovered Moffat. When Nannie wheeled her pram along the pavement few of those she encountered had ever seen a United States citizen.

She and Miss Syme chose their rooms with care and received courteous attention. From the windows they could look across to the Baths Hall, upgraded to the Town Hall. In the yard behind it a brand new Police Station had been built. Perhaps it was fortunate it had not been there when the soldiers and their girls spilled out on to the High Street during those wartime hops. Then the Station had looked over the school playing fields and the Sergeant had cultivated his garden between official duties. The mark left by the removal of the police insignia remained above that old house door still.

In the mornings Nannie and Miss Syme walked down to the Toffee Shop, much expanded and boasting a tearoom but still run by a grandson of old Mrs Blacklock, and selling Moffat Toffee to a worldwide market. Nannie, questioning the youth who served her morning coffee, heard him shout 'Dad, here's an old woman says she knew you when you were a small boy'. Such candour did not upset her. She was not nostalgic, and her lifework had been concerned with the development of new generations.

In one of the Council houses built on the fields opposite the boys' school Nannie H still lived. Jean, our cook, whose grandson was at Sandhurst, had a bungalow not so far away. One of the helpers in our kitchen in far off days, Mrs Boyce, who through family troubles and a frail physique had looked each year as though she would barely survive another winter, was still alive into a brisk old age. Wattie's only son was the pipe major in the Moffat band and *his* son, 'wee Ian', a dancer and singer with that band. Family names survived in fresh generations, with what was almost an historical connection with our own. The doctor – the young doctor in our day – was grey-haired now and retired, but Nannie knew him and he her; the current doctor had been at school with Laurence.

The wide High Street had hardly changed. It retained its distinctive character and offered splendid opportunities for informed speculation and discreet gossip. At one end the War Memorial now carried my brother Alastair's name; at the other the Ram on the fountain erected by William Colvin continued to snort proudly as it gazed southward. Moffat House Hotel, built by John Adam in 1762, gracious behind its circular approach, had watched the stage coaches driving up the High Street long before it saw my eve of wedding party. It surveyed the endless stream of buses still. If Nannie and Miss Syme felt affluent they could take afternoon tea in the elegant sitting room.

From those expeditions Nannie sent me postcards. One of them showed the Park, its small pavilion spic and span, red roof newly painted for the summer season, behind it the square tower of the parish church – which we had not attended – and the wooded mound of the Gallow Hill. There were fewer churches now, as there were fewer doctors and banks; some sources of rivalry had been eliminated.

Moffat House Hotel built c.1762

The church in which I had been married was replaced by a community theatre. Ducks and swans still paddled about the Park pond among the rowing boats and the rhododendrons beside the little bridge where Alastair had fallen in were fully grown. Only the flower beds had changed, meticulously kept with a profusion of blooms more magnificent than any I remembered. By the wall, next to the Beattock road, there was a memorial to Air Chief Marshal Lord Dowding of Battle of Britain fame, born in Moffat in 1882.

Beside the Park the station, from which we had gone those joyous journeys in the train, had disappeared. In its place was a motel, and behind that, in what had been the station yard, Moffat Weavers had their showroom next to the bus park, where long-distance coaches from the continent drew in beside Round Britain Tours and humbler Border Outings. Moffat Weavers had not existed in our day, now their name was known far and wide, due no doubt to the commercial acumen which had dictated the placing of a major outlet within easy reach of tourists debouching in their hundreds to set foot for the first time on Scottish soil. In the quieter reaches of the High Street, in what we had once known as Barrs, they had a second, up-market, shop.

The Black Bull, opposite the Parish Church, had become

respectable. Enlarged, harled in snow-white, it now recalled on a black plaque that it had been the headquarters of Claverhouse during the 'Killing Times'. Did this I wonder attract more customers in the 1980s than the romantic recollection of Robert Burns and his poem? Behind the inn the smithy still existed – with rows of Flymo lawn mowers hanging from its ceiling and never a horse in sight.

Usually Nannie would make an outing to The Lodge, walking slowly up Well Street, where the wartime canteen was now an antique shop and, although the name was still over the window, Hepburn's the bakers had passed to other hands. The Provost's shoe shop was empty, and in what had been Sinclair's, the grocer, there was a launderette. Past the corner where our old doctor's house stood the road used to open out as it went by the Masonic Hall, scene of our dancing classes, the prefabs built after the war, the mill with its horses and its pond. Here there were many changes. The prefabs and the mill were gone; the pond drained and filled in; a children's playground and rows of recently built houses crowded the fields beside which the burn ran.

Time had not dealt kindly with The Lodge after our departure. While we lived there it had seemed, whatever architectural deficiencies came to light, always the best and most felicitous of homes. For Nannie and my mother, wherever they subsequently went, it continued to be so. When we left it fell to pieces and it was years before the house managed to pick itself up again. I never went back to see it; but Nannie did, to people once again its garden with our shouts and laughter, to see my father's Minerva on the gravel sweep and my mother, handsome and smiling in the sunshine, on the front door step.

Most of the walks that Nannie had taken us in our childhood were too far now. Where once she had tripped lightly on the road to Holmend and Wattie's cottage then on to Rogermoor, or organised an expedition to see the ruins of the Hydropathic up Beechgrove, short breath and failing eyesight now curtailed her steps. Perhaps she hired a car to

run her up the Beef Tub road to the quiet cemetery where my
father and mother lay, and remembered on the way back
wild winter evenings when she sat beside my mother on the
drive home from Edinburgh. Or she contented herself with
shorter strolls, each with its memories, down to the park, or
up round the Crescent haunted still by the ghost of Mrs
Goldie-Boag.

In the last year of her life I went to Polmont to visit
Nannie, taking with me a tape-recorder. She knew I was
going to write a book about her and was excited by the idea.
Inspite of my protestations she insisted on giving me her
bedroom and herself going to sleep with a neighbour. In the
end I saw that it pleased her to fuss over me, as she had done
in the days when I was her child. She remembered the things
that I liked to eat, and her cooking, inspite of swollen finger
joints, was still excellent.

Afterwards we sat by the fire, Nannie with her back to the
light which her eyes could no longer tolerate. Between us,
on the table, lay the tape-recorder. At first she had been
apprehensive about this new-fangled instrument. I made her
talk a little, then rewound the tape and played her voice back
to her. Even in the shadow I could see the look of surprise and
pleasure that came into her large semi-blind eyes. Where
sitting with a notebook on my knee would have made her
nervous, absorbed in her own reminiscences she soon forgot
the little box.

That was the last time I saw her. She wanted to see the
book published, the record of the quiet life that she had found
so fulfilling made public. She never doubted that I could
make this happen. But it was not to be. Some months later
Robert telephoned to say that she was dead. Towards the
end, in the fullness of her eighty-six years, Nannie had lain
surrounded by the photographs of her children, and their
children, remembering happy days. When Robert went to
visit her, her face lit up. She murmured to her devoted niece
that there was no-one like her own family. At the last it was
not as Joanna Marshall that she spoke, it was as Nannie HR.

Once I had written to Nannie mentioning the making of my Will. The letter that came back surprised me. In it she commented on what I had said, but each time it became necessary to use the word 'Will' she left instead a blank. Remembering this superstition, I was astonished, when the time came, to find that she had made meticulous prior arrangements for her own funeral and had bought her plot in Moffat cemetery. Knowing that, some years before, I had lost all my table silver in a burglary she left me her teaspoons. She died, as she had always lived, independent and well organised, on the day Laurence's fifth grandchild was born. As was her custom, she had prepared a present for the coming baby.

We buried her in Moffat on a windy summer day. She lies just over a small hillock from my mother's grave. Afterwards, at her request, members of both her families went for a meal at Moffat House Hotel. Jean was there, and Wattie's son. So too was Mrs Boyce. Nannie's clever nephew assured me we had met before on the beach as infants though I could not remember. In the morning I had walked round the town, where memories of my childhood came flooding back. On every corner of Well Road and the High Street, Ballplay and the Park, I saw Nannie. On this day it did not seem sad that she was gone, rather there was a sense of resolution and fulfilment, of coming full circle. After a long life of loving and giving, Nannie had come home.

Golf Course

To BEATTOCK
& South

To Nannie F

Station   Park

River

Smithy   Black Bull   War Memorial

Andys
Garage

Shoes
Baker   Toffee
Shop

Grocer   Barr
Balm

Police   Well Rd

Dr.   The C

Duck Farm

Masonic Hall

Mill
Pond

The Lodge

Holmend   •Sch.

Wattie's
House

Ballplay

School
Ardenholm

Tennis

Rogermoor

To Grey Mare's Tail